VISITA INTERIORA TERRAE
RECTIFICANDO INVENIES OCCULTUM LAPIDEM

Zeit (f: v.i.t.r.ii.o.l.)

Patty Blanchfield

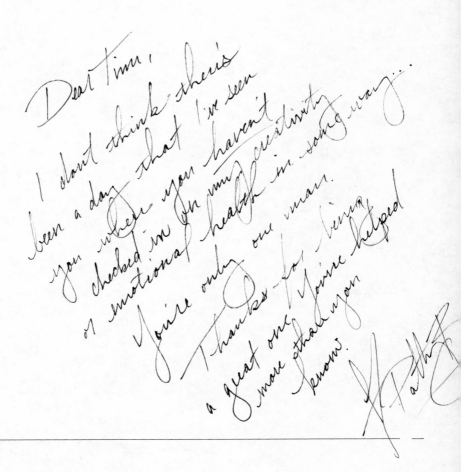

Dear Tim,

I don't think there's been a day that I've seen you where you haven't checked in on my creativity or emotional health in some way...

You're only one man.

Thanks for being a great one. You've helped more than you know.

Patty

I don't know you yet but my words will one day touch you and I need you to tell me how. I need you like the tide needs the wake; always a pull and then a push and we are both, in turn.

I need you like the Ocean needs the Moon.

I love you the way the Moon caresses the waves of the Sea in the early morning where their whispers are the only sound that's heard. If we were the Moon and the Sea we'd make love in the crashing of each diurnal tide unleashing a power kept nestled deep beneath'e waves...

VISITA

Calcination:
through fire the crow will become a dove

v.

Sometimes silence is orbital; what satellites can say elliptic until need for Language is overcome by a sense that two selves are once more out of sync.[1]

<u>Caput Mortuum</u>

So corporeal, this stolen breath
caught fresh between such broken lungs[2]
so fit, so lean
from clutching deep
in chains each cry resounds[3]

Prisoner bound to vanilla skies
soul hemorrhaging within my core[4]
all hope interred
as Horror flies
my faith in fire restored.

.20.3.12.

---

[2] Is there fire in my chest? This incessant burning, raging in half-held promises that blind me; it's the self subversion that preys upon my heart.
[3] Adrenaline is coursing through me in the riptide from this machine submerged in the afterbirth of aborted idea(l)s. What can I do?
[4] I'm lost and rendered, found wanting; smother me entirely till I'm black and blue in the face. I've given it up recently – living under your upper hand.

Bitter Pill

In words I am an heiress
yet sweet, so sweetly I come undone again
knees dirty before God

I took the blue pill tumbled smoothe in chrom(r)
        grope handed bent kneed fading in the mirror
                but can't see the Wonderland with the aubergine sky -
how long until it takes hold
o' me?[5] I'm a refugee splendid little thing,
and this wall, sentimental elephantine/
        my belly pregnant with regret and every little seed
    turned away bloody.
How many sins need be remembered?

dangerous gaze lover drink me in
        my oubliette
a crystal cave surrounds me interred in waking l,ife
        my coffin
        made of lips and eyes a naked sun swallows
in endless heaven I've got the shakes
sepulchral in reason my skin flakes tendons
poised/ right at
        my fingertips
holding on prevent me from wandering in tongues flickering –
        meant to be contained
but cobble shy/stack it up a suicidal staircase
        even further on the way down
till we're glancing epiphanies straight up in Harlem.

This day has all the grandeur of a rain cloud in Maine
and I could excuse every bitter reflection
were it not
for
the murmuring.

.28.9.12.

---

[5] Apathy is a disease.
Apathy is killing me. I could lose myself in my old ways:

Awake again. A solid week of this, my sole refuge – epiphanies must come in waves; they emerge such fitful dancers, falling to seizures on the stage. Presentation is the killer of dreams.

No one takes advantage of the serenity of this pier and it's just as well, for if they did, I'd stop coming here. The moonlight, my deep draught of consequence but no two footprints are the same on this muddy ground – must mean no one else bothers to return.

I need a pressure release; the ways I kill my self with every blue moon[6] are becoming a mythology.

I am feral in this darkness.

I want to breathe smoke.

.30.10.12.

---

[6] My lips are broken and bleeding, they've been so hazardous these days. Rose petals in bloom like bitten strawberries and no intoxicating mouth to contain each breathless scream.

The pipes clank in this carriage house. A steady and reverberating *twang!* that gently nestles between the floorboards below as tiny footprints above echo in scurried fury. The rain berates each window as if in reminder before burrowing deep within the sand, glistening in answer on the rocks, creating crystals bursting in their colourful disturbance before drifting, receding, disappearing like sacral wisdom into the mists that have unfolded each gnarled branch and fallen star in an ethereal vapour, thick and intimate in this gently falling darkness.

This silence deafening; hyper senses pull me into a trance. I am filled with clarity. Yet void, naturally, of any – if not transient – legitimate words to say. Just instinct without tangible – or phœnetic, rather – form.[7]

.27.2.13.

---

[7] I don't know who he's going to be today.

I have no voice.

A burning strain builds within my lungs, closing my throat before I can speak; clouds descend into my eyes. I cannot lift them to meet yours, to watch you penetrate the fugitive cabaret that is perception versus rehearsed disdain and impose what you feel I've become as all I've given in confidence you flaunt to ridicule.

I have no voice.

All sound stops before each withered thought can manifest – they would echo in this sore and aching silence growing to fill the house with concealed intentions; harsh concavity for my part, withheld, before the damage can be done.

I have no voice.

The water pounds in a needling barrage as the scourge you remind me I should feel I deserve for my thoughtless negligence – my sex was programmed to receive and you insert insidious remnants of your self within my Visage you depend upon in validation – and the panic leaves you drowning in delusion as my heart is merely a reliquary of the love I pray to when your mania forgets my face.

I have no voice.

You swear you need this invasion to feel secure – your sex was programmed to infect me – and I have nothing to hide but you swear my word is suspect unless I give them to pages you can see; incriminate my will in order to vindicate your own though I swear you prefer me as an idea unrealized as a world away you cling to me but when I'm right here and I touch you your eyes never meet mine.

I have no voice.

---

[8] An impulse suspended, sacrosanct, needling into my pores like a scarab, engulfing and consuming me.

I have no voice.

A daily mantra of, "This is the mark she left on you." This fear of yours has to be soothed but when you first crept inside me it felt foreign and it's been a feeling I cannot shake.

Intimacy without intimacy but we are intimately involved and there's no proof I could cite without crippling your pride, again, in a way I do not intend.[8]

Ma'at

I leave art in my mirror, rehearsed. Remote.
Suspend every emoted fear, in sub-sequence of "truth,"
the conversions flawless and I put another pebble on the scale.

My heart is gone from me. Gone until I'm dead and even.
Now, my blood –
it's thickening again
a coursing wave of oil tinged with venom — *When did I breathe in fire?*
rising and falling in the beat of my tumultuous tides.
I feel the vibrato in the pull of every consequence surging
      through my veins,
pressing deep and pooling in the hollow.
      I left a single name there: his.[9]
My breasts burden me.
They ache and swell sporadic in vicious memento;
I fill them,
hard,
but I am drowning in this air
I beat them make them listen, but there's an echo deep inside
Overpowering every word
to drop the last veil.

.9.4.13.

---

[9] Any attempt at meditation today has resulted in the persistent image of needles protruding from my eyes or skin as if imprinted on the back of my eyelids.

Their Turn

I've heard it said that when people begin to approach the end of their lives it comes on slow, like a fever; that fever, rising, becomes inevitability,[10] and the only sensible thing to do is wait.

Wait for the end. Wait for an opening in time.

The lucky ones are chauffeured to see their grandchildren as they laugh and play and whine, running breathless across the floorboards while their quiet posts[11] rest gently on cushioned chairs. A frenzied world running wild as they patiently stay to watch, carefully, for just a little while. Just a little while. Absorbing all the tiny smiles and eyes wide as Christmas orbs – brighter than any star.

The lucky stick around to watch, adding to a lifetime of memories with a silent, gentle smile. Content rehearsing as shades before the Big Day. Quiet limbs slowly coming to rest like willows in a dying wind.

Her tired eyes seek mine and linger as she pulls in another rattling breath. Her smile is slow, but spreads, and I know she's thinking of me as a little girl tearing through the trees at the Fort, hungry as an Indian for a little danger as I lorded over my bastion and I think, *if Grandpa were here he'd laugh, open his hands wide to the room and say, "This is important,"* because every memory with family is a moment we'd immortalize in a story portraying the myriad ways in which an Irishman can be clever and recount them, with every meeting, in the hopes that repetition would soothe her trembling memory, in the hopes that repetition would make every witness an orator, in the hopes that repetition would ensure the generations remember as the years wear on so every story is recounted in a familial meeting place and we can almost forget that those that we remember are no longer here.

If Grandpa were here, he'd ask every girl, "Shall we dance?" when they converge steps in hallways, "Because dancing is the only thing to do with a pretty girl's feet," in apology for almost stepping on them.

---

[10] I could summarize the past few months with nothing but the sound of cauterizing skin. but I won't.

[11] Sentient sentinels on the fringe of the scene, gently watching.

But he isn't here and though the scenes are set he doesn't enter and though his cues are laid before us he doesn't speak and he isn't here and though she forgets sometimes I can see in her eyes that today, in the silence, is a day that she remembers. And he isn't here but we sit in temple silence watching them make new memories in this house without him.

She takes a slow, shaky sip of tea,
nods in their direction
and tells me,

"Their turn."

.14.5.13.

S[[ocial/SN]] Media

Anyone with a camera and a mirror is a model, gracing the covers of their own borrowed pages. Deep within these social constructs and pre-formatted *journales* all we do is fill in the blank space with imprints of our recent Self.

The world is ours, a sea of possibility for creativity and self-expression, as long as the **share** button works.

Selfies and framed reflections through a filter distinguish us from public eye and as each serpentine thought is clouded in noble imagery, we get away with murder.

Once we press **delete.** Once we press **private.** Once we **block** inconvenient perceptions.

We're all models now and the creases and curvature of our skin subsists on revolutions seen by Armani, Vervatos and Wang, or at least that's what our search algorithms would lead us to believe – we're on commission, treading the catwalks lined in flashing lights and house music waiting for our cues to hit the camera with a fierce gaze; each profile a magnum opus sucking on the lips of delirium in a shrouded den.

Models. Perfection incarnate of some carnal ruse or another. Our legacy for the world after. Leeches will bleed us in the final cut but, for now, we are immortal.

.12.7.13.

Potatohead

I wasn't born with it.
I'm more of a Mr. Potatohead
with adornments adhered[12]
to my face
& hands
& legs
& waist
you can easily remove.

You can easily replace.

I wear lipstick now
to match the red
from where I'm biting my lip
or you're kissing me.
But only one happens now.
There's a pulse I adopt[13]
where I can slip through time,
through walls;
you'd look in my eyes & see nothing at all.[14]

Leave a legacy of stale breath like it's the last trick you'll ever perform.[15]

Make the executive decision to disappear.[16]

---

[12] Someone took the plastic off my life and all the discarded layers of skin from the people in it are turning to dust and getting in the cracks.

[13] There's a lunar-powered metronome in the corner creating its own time signature from scattered memories of the sound it makes when broken.

[14] A portrait hangs on the wall with a blank space fit for a name, never to come in contact with this dust or be removed from its frame.

[15] Sometimes I read your words as a substitute for "getting to know each other."
Sometimes I read mine as a substitute for fiction.

[16] we have to find our way back once we get there because
everywhere we find ourselves is a place we feel we've already decided not to go

INTERIORA

Dissolution:
from the ashes a flood will spring,
carrying the seed of the soul

i.

Anger is the sheath
we wear around the heart
to protect us
from the pain of Truth.

The pendulum is burrowing deep beneath'e sands of time; its path is etched in high relief creating little dunes of destiny to cradle the oscillating scale.

.28.3.12.

?5\4 avril2012[17]

I left him there,
a shrinking gargoyle of the citadel,
aghast and sputtering.
All his yesterday's filleted across a splintering mind's eye
milky as a spider's web
and every point connected.
No sight is worth a thousand deaths
no genii can extinguish;[18]
Transpose, instead, a memory of mornings brimming
casteless beauty extended to the sky.
At his feet I laid my Hope exalted;
My burning offering
that preyed upon me weightless
as the doves whispered canticles of gracious lullabies
falling from his lips creating life
where I had lost the memory.[19]

Protected hearts shake from every sound
of majesties distorting their only empires
his city r[[e(ai)g]]ning flames I could never prophesy
my body turned to salt at the very sight
as he lay there, twisted prayers[20]
invoking the Passion that might egress
immortal fears æternal.

---

[17] qu'est-ce qu'aujourd hui?
le matin, fraud comme mon ciel;
malade, comme mon coeur.
[18] *hands captured desperate*
fallen and saviour – does he know who he's become?
does he know who he is to me?
in his eyes
an inner light
in his voice
a tender smile
for one precious moment
before the little lights
went
out.
[19] I am Jack's stolen breath.
[20] He told them I was an angel.

Vignettes

I'm a film critic, these days.
Starring as my own hopeless ingénue
in vacant need for vacancy
pausing, stopping all my vignettes
till the dialogue's a little tighter, the blocking sweeps
and flows into the next scene flawless, seamless –
Marquee of yellow lights down every barren street.
My soundtracks will make you bleed.

There, that corner, is where we botched
fight call, and each regretted line
listless and strained; we could have blown out
every streetlamp – showered in pearls and embers –
but we held back and fucked all the cues
and no one had to yell "Cut!" when it was silent
because I knew.

Now I've locked myself in my dark room
editing the shit out of your face on this film.
I'll blow the contrast down
till this red letter on my flawless record is muddy
partial and riven
the lines of your cheek are juxtaposed in smoke.

No saturation, sync the film noir filter:

The Unknown Man fading slowly into silhouette –
That secret smile? Cut and lost
quickly dissolving into cellophane I finally see through.

Don't even bother to laugh – don't taste so bitter –
because the sound's cut too.
I just refuse.
But I'll leave the burn marks on the reel
just to remember how it feels
that thirty seconds before the cut and dry.[21]

---

[21] I can't see, my eyes are pinked, and I'll dig at these scars till I'm blind. Till my skin's just as pockmarked as my mind.

Without those eyes
I'd be invincible.

.4.10.12.

Without those eyes, I'd be invincible.

I could ruin mine in this failing light.[22] There are days when I'm fading and completely without fire, but my heart rages on within my chest.

It must be instinct that drives me to this place. A storm could snuff out every desperate lantern, yet I'd still lay quiet, softly trembling by the riverside and halting my every breath to match the whispering waves in tantric reminder.

What am I that must train myself to breathe again? Why am I so contained? A river doesn't wait, it rises and falls according to the tide, each pulse collecting sand, each wave exchanging foam.

There is something calming about this chaos. I could scream and shake with rage and it's nothing this river hasn't seen before. My heart could break and my body lose form and maybe I'd feel as if I'd accomplished something intrinsic, something insightful and raw, and the melody of this breeze drifting over its patient lover just so, like a breath when their head is resting gently on your chest...

It wouldn't change.

What can I do? What is there to say. I came to the River realizing how much I stand to learn. How far I still have to go. Through it all, it isn't peace I'm searching for, no. I could speak volumes giving that impression, I'm told, but I live through my desires because as much as I admire the Truths and the Wheel I crave only what I lack which means I crave my own perfection without miasma stopping my breath like the shore misses the waves without the sickness that we leave poisoning its depths and this poignant chaos starves me like a babe without a tit because if this existence bred me for Heaven then I wouldn't have a reason to live because anytime I find peace I find that I want nothing more. And contentment is complacency.

I cannot stay here. This River, this night tells me my pain is not yet over. There is more that I must do. My faith scares you because yours remains consistently unchanged.

It is my Mother's Milk because my mother does not deal in Truth unfairly.[23]

The Truth is that Beauty is of my own design: I can pine, I can want, I can give words like a fountain but I can never be whole, human and my own self. Happiness[24] is not for the likes of me.

---

[22] *I'm sure that's something my mother would say.*

[23] *Is Truth ever beautiful? Is Beauty ever Truth?*

[24] Truth and Happiness feel as a solution akin to oil and water. Greatness, though... Greatness requires blood. Blood will mix with both.
What am I.

Firsts of Many

She read away the morning in a turnstile haze;
lost and burning old fires for light.
What a prison Time can be sometimes as it passes too quickly;[25]
buried in the confines of this foreign and familiar house.

The sun lazily dripped in frozen crystals from the sky coating the ground
in white.
Candles gently flickering an amber glow upon the walls
and she waited.

If Time could not be patient, she would be. Sometimes it stole her
memories. Sometimes it gave them back.[26] The memories glistened in the
corners of her down-turned eyes and she inhaled deeply a temporary
silence as what she thought she knew disappeared again and now she had
to wait to remember what it is she'd just forgotten.

Porcelain angels danced within the tabernacles nestled in the hall,
everything polished in crimson and green silently singing in an ethereal
echo. The praise of one consumed by love and fear — a single branch of
mistletoe hung low from the chandelier.

So this, she thought, *This is what another First feels like. And they all thought it
impossible to live two moments as one; on the edge of temporal existence, of
liminal form, I am still caught in a love so young and so wise.*

First Christmas with, all those years ago, blushing. First Christmas without, and
her heart was silent, *A life together staying, fading, straying past the boundary
of a half-remembered dream…*

Footsteps betrayed a form from down the hall.

Tired eyes so young and full, same as her own in all but colour —
experience betrayed in years — blinked away the morning light.
"Good morning, dear," she said. "I would have made coffee, but I've
forgotten how."
"I am *on* it, then," the girl hid both eyes behind a smirk. "You like it how
you like your men?"[27]

---

[25] like the ones you love.
[26] returned as prodigal images in a flash of love and pain.

"You? But. Well, where's the maid?"

"I'm the… stand-in," the young girl said. "Merry Christmas, Grandma."

.26.12.12.

---

[27] *Good joke. Everyone laugh.*

Siren

How quickly needles seal the eyes with
their sharp tug.
Wax can insulate the ears,
poison coats the tongue in silence
when necessity deems it so,
co-existing.

When the right chords just won't play,
fingertips brush the skin behind his neck,
and whispers just aren't enough[28]
but pries and pleads
get nowhere
puncturing the pressure pointed
passion play –
these oubliettes fit like a glove.

I'll be wandering blind and fitful
;sleep comes for those who rest –
in peace we find ourselves
undone together.
give us time enough.

These oubliettes fit like a glove;
give us time enough.

---

[28] Say, "ethereal echo" with me in as many ways as you can, rearranging emphasis so each genesis of one word affects the other in desperate attempt to suspend ugliness: Ethereal echo. Ethêræl ēcho. Æthéreal èchó…

Friday the 13th

Another breath,
      Another step.
Jettisoned back to Ground Zero.
The blood won't flow
      if you
      cauterize
the font of
pain's [[in/con]]ception.

But I can't fit the dremel into that particular valve
because the skin already scarred is tougher than the skin
that is now creasing.
I'll drown it.[29]

Forget me.

.13.9.13.

---

[29] The veil is thin here; thin enough to slip through time and be gone before you remind me how little she was supposed to mean to you.

I'm walking on broken ground. An acrid tincture squeezes blood from my tongue to leave me muted in situ.[30] Waiting to be usurped.

To my body I am xeno and we are at war.

My skin is a porous tomb and I am heavy with the clinging fog, aching with the strain of bones breaking their better natures not to run from this place.

Some days I can't stand to be so accessible. Voice is an instrument serving the heart's melody to lovers; it is inexcusable for that melody to be served unkempt and out of time.

---

[30] My head is Total Recall splitting, starting with the eyes, and the room prefers to spin in panoramic view.

Sol[[o]]

He sets an alarm every morning.
Full volume and heavy bass,
"To give you
something to wake up to," he says.
I sleep through it every time. Drifting through the deep
calm in the æther of my dreams,
contented,
safe in the arms that held me there
as morning creeps in through the window.
Until he rests his hand on my chest
with the slightest push
And leans into me, gently
In a breath whispering, "Hey…"
And I can see that I am awake in the
reflection of his eyes
As we lay there, eyes open.
As I lay there, wanting to be held.
I taste the warmth in the breath he has exhaled
and smile.
I can see that I am smiling.

Sometimes I'm quiet, angel.
It's not you, I just.
I don't trust myself to speak.
Sometimes I'm afraid the words will dissolve as they escape me.[31]
Dissolution through searing pipes, vapourous.
Meaning versus intention;
transubstantiation of words into tears.
This is my body
and this is my blood
and you insist though it's sacrilege to eat it.

.30.10.12.v.

---

[31] That ain't Art in my Mirror and it's not my body that curses you.

There's a bat in my ceiling. Seems fitting considering the terrain outside; the sky is dead and dreary. Every tree has become void of vibrancy and colour.[32]
Silhouettes interrupting empty space.
It's the same in here, but. Ya know.
I have the heat on.

.11.11.14.

---

[32] The amount of tears I've let fall on your shirt are nothing compared to what I've shed inspired by you.

Buckle

I often struggle
in moments
when it's important
for me
to be firm in my convictions
that it's not actually just ok.

Be it
timing
or place

hard to say
vs.
hard to hear –[33]
I have to struggle not to buckle.

If I took the time
to thank everyone
who *made me who I am,*
I'd waste too much time
giving too many people
too much
fucking
credit.[34]

.1.11.14.

---

[33] How fitting that the day you lost your love was the day it began to grow inside me.

[34] Dissolution is as far as you're ever gonna get, girl. Crystallized thoughts, repressed.

Snow

Monday I named you; Friday you were gone.[35]

the steps I trace are in time with the undulations of a dull knife losing teeth under a long, slow drip; full moons are my kill switch to fold in, collapsing bone into sinew, snapping fast as butterflies, until my whole self fits in the dry sockets within two careful blinds.

harsh light bleeds in but I weigh nothing here as I hide from this lantern bleeding argent vapour, drifting in, but I am not my body. I am enclosed within this temple merely a reliquary to be sent away to bury. I am not my swollen breasts that can't remain, this bitter taste of rotting oil from the machine that is my hips. I am none of these things, but still, the Moon, she steals from me.

I am not my body within this temple, I am not my heart that sinks deep in its own chasm deflating lungs with no will of their own to recognize when they are empty without the code that reminds them to inhale, I am not this ghost hidden in my mouth that without my lungs only gives forth a silent scream.

I will remain in this temple, nameless and without time, a hollow banal thing creeping from crevice to precipice, tearing at what skin I have borrowed to contain an obsolete pairing of organs encased in bone to keep the rigor from infecting my spine.

---

[35] *you can't miss what you don't know and you'll never know the cadence he hums when the silence is comfortable; the subtle curve of his bottom lip reaching the corner of his mouth serving to prophesy the wave of each irreverent eyelid. you can't miss the vibrato of his breathing or the grand production as he orchestrates each chime of the bell tower falling from the sky with a maestro's prestige, placing them where he believes they belong. you can't miss the ache in your bones wondering whether he means it today. he says he wouldn't have wanted you to know him, asking to be released from the pain of your loss in absolution of love, which, to him is only a burden. above all, this is the one truth I am grateful to protect you from; this is the way you stay loved the entirety of your gentle minutiae of life. you can't miss a love that was only ever conditional, wondering how you missed that fact all this time, watching him crave and obsess over each unconquered thing until the moment he feels guilty for possessing it, placing it in a configuration ready to be purged.*

you can't miss my counting each silken follicle and training them to rest in accordance with each caress or planting just as many kisses as the number I'd have committed to memory, plus ten for every finger and toe.

but I will.

your heart would have beat like a bird's but mine is a forgotten stone that aches when it rains.

slide my tongue back in my mouth when I stop shaking;

scrap the rest for parts.

.28.6.16.

Is there a prayer one might whisper to invoke a gentler mind? Some incantation to incite the wake of a slumbering sea whose winds have retreated to their Æolian chamber, having razed the surface of a despondent coast irreparable, leaving an emptiness within a mere reflection of stars that drifts in the echo of inimitable silence –

The pulse I rest in is one of peace attained solely by the obedient absence of the storm complacent in a quiet that is borrowed, not to mention shallow in effect, affecting each tender sinew I claim as my own as the tendrils of memory spiral into antiquity.

Every breath occurs within a reliquary as dispassionate as it is disused, a foreign amphora to be emptied, existing in quadrants, struggling for necessity.[36]

To what compound fracture of self can I attribute these insufficiencies?

My machine is the Xeno that inspires insurrection.

.30.8.16.

---

[36] Hell hath no fury.

It is merely an existence without Love.

Whirligigs

This song is for you
though you'll be vacant this year.

We all believed you were finished playing a part
but sometimes
the masques we wear are the only things we hold onto
when the edge becomes the hope:
the prayer we cling to.[37]

You can't read the words you write until you've written them
just as you can't learn from your mistakes until you've made them
but the hands you used in prayer
are now the hands he wants to rest inside,
the hands to which he'll always compare his own
he'll clasp, unclasp around her hair
and in his eyes reflected crystals coat the ground outside
and your voice
the one he mimics in the mirror
is the one he'll never hear
save but a precious echo just before dawn
where dreams still linger.

He cannot know how empty the world will be without you,
though the winds will change
leaves drifting from the trees in patient order
to make room for the sky to fall,
until the memory returns
that you are gone.

Somehow we'll always forget that you are gone.

And in a whisper

:because it hurts for it not to be a secret:

we'll pray
:because in your last years it meant so much to you that we pray:

---

[37] I refuse anything I might have become other than precisely who I am right now
but I've come to realize how little I knew of who I was at the time of my being.

and we'll plead,

:because it isn't a curse so much as a creation of wholes from parts
of both fiction and fact that are beyond our understanding:

"Goddamnit, baby
we were here."[38]

.1.11.16.

---

[38] Medieval alchemists believed the salt in tears was the actual remnant of crystallized
thoughts broken down by crying, like a frozen wave splintered into shards crashing to the
shore slow, but unyielding, and always in shifts.

The only sound heard is the echo of a gently breaking bell.

It was symbolism for our dead generation.

TERRÆ

Separation:
the wind carries the soul at war within its belly

_t._[39]

*All that's left of us is
all that's left of us
and me:
invading your demeanour
and you:
yielding to it.*

---

[39] / telos.

Broken Arrow

The snow fell to bury us this year.[40]

This season too dead to stay inside.

We drove to an hotel on the North side of town, smoke trailing behind us from the hookah bar, harDCore heralding our entrance on the scene from the two speakers that worked.

Rose and I, Mirror and his brother – on leave from the Army – just on the cusp of late and early. No one here to check us in, we scaled the fence just under the Big Brother camera and uncovered the hot tub.

The steam turned the frozen air into a thickness we could hold in both hands.

They wasted no time, pants off before Rose and I could avert our eyes, and his brother said, "Come on, Echo; this was your idea," as I hesitated chiaroscuro, as I thought about taking my shirt off in front of anyone other than Mirror; I'd only been down to mismatched lingerie when the lights were off hoping his hands, his eyes, his lips wouldn't linger too long on the folds of my skin too harshly illuminated in the liquid light of the moon.

I looked to him as if to ask, "You solid with him sharing me?" as he shrugged and settled beneath the rippling water.[41]

Rose was wearing her bright red bra and I envied her supple D's, thin legs and protruding stomach that gave her honest hips an hourglass and a femininity I never had. Just aching muscles always maxed and the fat that collects over time; no breasts or hips, just black band shirts and pants that never fit.

---

[40] *No matter where we go*
lights pass us in the street
in shooting orbs
that leave us drunk;
our vision as suspect
as our intentions.
At 18 you own nothing but
conviction and the night.

[41] "Love is a broken arrow bent on destruction and chaos; the only constant thing about Love is that it is absolute murder on the heart that harbours it."

I pleaded her with a face as I unhooked my belt, a face that asked, "We keeping the bras on?" and she laughed as out loud I said, "Because, fuck," and she smirked a glance in big brother's direction. It's hard to call someone a future stepmom with a look, but I succeeded and she flipped me off and when I peeled my shirt off it wasn't as cold as I'd imagined.

I'll walk this wasteland with you.

You know that thing assholes do when they start pulling their pants down before taking off their shoes? That was me, hippity hopping like a fuck, untying my Chucks to the truncated tune of *Out of Step* relentlessly sounding off in my head.

When I finally made it to the water I was laughing and almost forgot who was in the tub, the water slicing my skin off in long sheets replacing my legs with needles and heat.

I looked up and Mirror and brother had their arms stretched over the side, eyes locked and intent on drinking me in. I hugged my arms and dipped my chin to my chest to let my hair blanket me in a sheltering silhouette, uncertain what to cover as the needles invaded the tender skin of my stretch marks that raged across my hips and thighs.

"I see why you like her," brother said, tapping Mirror's shoulder, and when his eyes finally met mine he gave me a wink as if I was welcome.[42]

I turned to Mirror, trying to find his eyes for something that said I was more than that, as I slouched so the water would cover my shoulders, burning my skin because I sat too fast, steam suffocating me because I can't breathe in water mixed with chlorine, the sound of the bubbles roaring in my ears drowning the conversation that existed without and around me creating the normalcy that I couldn't exist in, feeling his glares as a palpable entity, jealous I could engage his brother in more meaningful conversation about the hierarchy of punk music and the marriage of aesthetics within fine art and ancient history than he could, though he tried, though I had no interest in his brother, though he stayed awake while I slept to talk to me in my sleep to make sure.

Mirror wouldn't look at me.

---

[42] Either everyone is wrong or the dysmorphia is real.

When we left I blew a kiss to the cameras just before flipping Big Brother off and sat silent in the backseat feeling my hair slowly freeze in icy tendrils that would become both nimbus and weapon against his perceptions of me.

.23.12.07.

Tiptoe, Oneiros,

to keep me at rest and dreaming.
How softly your son plays his ambrosiac song,
a sentinel at the door
giving pennies till they're cold
to every soul caught between the Crossroads
and the River
wide-eyed in noumenon.

I suck my pomegranate seeds gently in reminder
of the sweet vermouth
I took from his tongue as he swore
he could rest his weary head
on my perfect breasts
forever
and we both lay silent
uncertain whether he meant to say anything at all.[43]

Believe everything and nothing that leaving men say.

If I'm a guiding light
he'd be a knife in the dark[44]
and I may never read his words again
but my name rests in the margin[45]
where he led me back to death
insatiable.

I left him lying
entombed in the Morning Bell.

.14.3.12.

---

[43] I always let men off the hook this way
[44] because I didn't mean to find him there
every song I sang a dirge for a name now silenced
no one here could ever know
and he thought it odd how many Manhattans I drank without faltering
but he ate every cherry I left untouched on the bar,
gently painting his tongue and lips in bourbon dripping,
as I left mythologies encased in his eyes for safe keeping.
[45] re: "Your character emulates Domitian." [[I can't remember if I wrote Diocletian instead.]]

Crossroad [[B&]] Blues

Do you need proof that I'm alive again? I'm settled by the bar a half-second stall permeating through the guts of conversation – I have every slick dream memorized from chemical stares borrowed from the lab; they keep me suicidal but only in the mornings. What is this gentle hunger taming my very will?

God left me a damned and broken child – I recognize the scent of sin, but not its opiate taste. How quickly will I fall unmatched, in sanctioned siren's filigree, as I make my way through Hell?

A diplomat they've made of me.[46]

Compound me to the core: it's where I belong though you'd never believe me if I told you; this soul entrenched in embalming fluid the only way it bends and swells alive. I am Fate's unwilling flower,[47] fixed and fickle, at this makeshift gate.

This scene would choke maggots. His bloated sex and lips at your throat gives pause to unwelcome strangers at the cusp of faith and vellum coated garters; I close my eyes against his creeping fingers you refuse to either clasp or turn away but I'm not leaving till these fucks make love to their microphones and these punks that brood in hyacinth moods give a smile to me they didn't intend.[48] I'd have this power normally but the hops just make it easy.

An hemlock taste to this cannibal kiss, un-medi(c)ated:

fool is: fair is: fragile :: cast incompetent airs.

I can't pretend to h(a)unt their cognizance.

I am flawed.

---

[46] Sync and carry low this restless heart you find, a carrion affair. Do you see me massacred in headlights the way I see myself? No? Then you're not looking hard enough. I swear you've got this all wrong – I swear I won't be around for long.
Don't take me for a bleeding heart, cause I'll take you for an hurricane.
[47] Granting immortality at the expense of brotherhood.
[48] You may stop there; all I want is conversation.

No one intrigues me here.

Dear Jimmy,
The Crossroads sucked tonight.
I bugged Kenny about the whiskey for you
but the Devil
never
showed
up.

At a precipice of Ifs, Nows and Whens,
so many photographs of what could be
flashing derelict deceits
in time
with the endless thundering
in my brain.[49]

Instead of heads
I collect hearts,
a capricious Bluebeard of my age,
and they are all of them so eager
even in the face
of my express warnings.

Resting their heads upon the cavern
where my heart should be –
do they just pretend to hear an heartbeat?[50]

There's no conspiracy
these wandering limbs could uncover
yet they sleuth
and search
and devour me.

.22.10.12.

---

[49] I am so damn tired of this relentless game.

[50] My animus wishes for my heart to be mechanical; for a man to Create he must first bury himself inside and though she pleases him in death, she will be resented for every piece he leaves inter[[r/n]]ed.

I Like it With the Door Closed

I don't sleep much. It is not so much a question of *"Why?"* as it is, *"What would I rather be doing…?"*

And in the solace of each cavernous night I discover the part of myself that is quiet and reserved, veering for the shadows. Praying, silently, for the impenetrable shield of anonymity where I realize the answer is, *"So. Many. Other. Things."*

Those which remain impossible in the daytime; coming and going in the wake of the next checked box on the list, we are uncertain as to where we are really meant to stay at any given moment. And at the end of the day, what do we do? Voices all around rushing us out or holding us up, down the next alley where you grip your keys in your hands and walk faster than you intend to admit, unaware of whether it was the feeling or the sound that unearthed your spine and stopped your breath, coming in through the trees when you thought you were alone and down the hallway creeping over your skin and behind your ears and before you know it their conversation is all you can hear or think or believe and you just want to go, anywhere, just to be Away.

There's a part we play in the light. A socialite sense of self sheathed in protection. We are constantly bundled up, against the elements, against each other, against ourselves[51] and when we remain, wherever we are, we have one foot prepared to exit and one eye outside the door and when we leave it is a practice for those we'll leave behind and coming back we sit behind who we were yesterday watching our selves expecting an answer as we sit knowing who we are is who we wanted to be realizing who we

---

[51] We wear:
dated hats to cover our ears
warm scarves around our tender necks
frayed jackets for our cringing shoulders
stained shirts to keep our hearts intact
ripped jeans to protect our sex
h[[a/o]]llowed gloves for our shaking hands
tattered shoes on our aching feet
layers of lipstick to leave evidence because
we have to find our way back once we get there because
everywhere we find ourselves is a place we feel we've already decided not to go
so we go but when we get there we've already left behind our thoughts of
what's ahead of us is
what's ahead of us;
what's ahead of
what's ahead?

are wishes we had wanted something different then so maybe we'd be them instead.

.6.1.13.

Phantom Limb

You were so anxious this morning – all night, flurrying from one side of the bed to another, my lips furiously smothered in yours and gone before I had the chance to wake, neck wet with *I'm sorry, I'm sorry*s in breathy mantras cascading over me like sand as our borrowed time slipped away from us and I just wanted you to hush and kiss me so I could pretend we wouldn't have this *last morning* to feel alive before flying home and you wouldn't hold onto the guilt of my tears until the next time we're here.[52]

Isn't life under the sun just a dream?[53]

I want to exist, weightless, my only connection to this corporeal plane at the edge of your kiss.

I want poverty and hunger subsisting on writing and creativity until we've lost everything resembling comfort and can rebuild ourselves into our truest forms, no miasma of useless attachments clouding our resolve for greatness, nothing but our brilliance ensuring we never want for money or love again.

I want to be inspired by dirty streets and pain and just by coming *home*.

 [[to you?]]

I want sweat and wine and bloodstains on the bed.

If you don't know I've already forgiven you before you ask then you've never seen the pain in your own eyes and baby, hell, we've been over this:

---

[52] I know it's panic. I know you love me and I will believe everything you see fit to say in the calm, I just.
One day I need you to tell me what you mean and what you don't.
[53] I love you. Just let me.
And I hear you, without escalation.
I tell my mirror when you're gone, "If I learn how to help, it won't hurt anymore; this ugliness is only temporary."
But sometimes I just don't know how to be.

I'll be strong for us now, eating your sins as they fall and I'll work your aching heart in my mouth, tongue invading each forbidden balcony of you hidden from view[54] and when I return it to you it will be smaller than you remember without the enteric coating of vitriol calcified after years of disuse.

.28.7.13.

---

[54] When your heart floats like a feather
and you can sleep without guilt pressing
on your chest as an hag –
then.
then you hold me;
until then
I'm holding you.

But I'm not your mirror
and I'm not her.
I'm the one who's right here;
why am I the last person you see?

Origin

The Joker took my story literal; a patient martyr in the mirror.
In situ, I see a silhouette with heaving breasts, but no eyes, no fire inside –
a coerced façade giving every corner solace.

There are creases in my skin I don't remember.
Around the eyes.
Around the mouth.

I see the world spin around me through a double-paned glass bell jar
where *Spectator* becomes a papier mâché face I wear, temporarily, when I
just don't have the words.

All sounds become a murmuring, a whirl of activity played out in gentle
montage pressing glimpses behind my eyes I can revisit later, sobering[55] as
all pressure is a blinding light constrained.[56]

.3.7.13.

---

[55] unwavering expansion; all hearts within the mold

[56] Quiet reminders echo in the dark.

Pantheon

a noxious terror in my lungs
gives birth to crippled ideals[57]

Mirror, mirror, you be kind
these precedents are borrowed
and this countenance could be my last.

I've sacrificed to epiphany
when I shook the earth
and my mind was gone from me
in temple silence.

My only oculus is gripping floor;
trampling darkness with truth
but the shadows grow
as the light in the nooks and apses fade.

An abscess grows in the shade.

And day after day the light shifts and stays;
shadows grip my face no matter how I turn away.

All I can do is wait when darkness fills the room.

In a moonless night of pitch and the last candle spent,
last resorts incite a prayer for another sunrise.[58]

.6.9.13.

---

[57] It is ill-advised to swim within two hours of complete emotional upheaval.
[58] The world never ends when it's supposed to.

Things I Want Written On My Tombstone:

.:. Her wiggle was too strong.

.:. Now I'm an evolved motherfucker,
but I'm about to get real fresh here in a second.

.:. Sometimes I bury myself,
realize I'm being lazy
with some aspect of my life
and wake up
with the answer
staring me in the face
as if it lived there.
Oh hi, Clarity,
I didn't see you there…

.:. Words are slow.:.2.47.9.23 .:.

.:. I am something other than human.

.:. Slide my tongue
back in my mouth
when I stop shaking;
scrap the rest for parts.

.:. Yes, these are tears from writing.
Yes, I am comfortable with that.
I am Enlightened.

.:. How often
do we look past ourselves
in the mirror?
To see the world
as the world sees us?
Our image is our pain.
The world is our consequence.

.:. Music as the only means
to drown out the sound
of my own doubts
laid out ad nauseum;
to memory and alphabetically.

Without failing or fronting,
I hate who I fear I'll become.

.:. *"High-souled persons have two states*
like that of a bunch of flowers:
either they are on top of the world
or they should wither and die."

Hindu proverb.

.:. Everywhere that my words have been laid
is a tomb in which I've buried my self.

.:. My ribcage is a slaughterhouse.
I've got memories hanging from hooks.

.:.Sometimes I can't tell
whether it's my skin
or my touch
that feels foreign.

.:. Temporary dissonance
is not indicative
of self worth.[59]

.:. Dante in the streets;
Virgil in the sheets.

---

[59] If I had a vanity I looked into
at several moments every day
I'd pose two questions to myself
in the margins of my reflection:
First,
"What albatross are you carrying around your neck today?"
And then, inevitably,
"For whom?"

<u>RECTIFICANDO</u>

Conjunction:
from War will come a Great Marriage,
a crucifixion of the Anima and Spiritus

r.

Fresh air invades the last demeanor left;
one breath escapes, soft as hidden teeth,
to fill a cavern that once remained in vigil silence.
"Revel in your time."

Be::epheron

Perfection cannot bare children;
we are every bit as stable as a flame.

Sometimes I imagine the stone melting
and you would laugh
arms wild about me so I wouldn't shake
but I'd still writhe like a captured beast
in frenziac protest of my brimming shame
volcanic in fervour
yet miasmic to my heart
immersed in flames; his wisdom plagues me.[60]

How quiet death is
yet my mind is riotous.
In hubris I wish them to compare
in some manifestation of form
reflecting the shattered emblems
imprinted in the fired glass.

.17.4.12.

---

[60] *What did your Father teach you?*

Vendetta di Venere

Stepping carefully onto the cold, sepulchral shore, the boy with a coin settled in against the wind – so busy making sails out of his shirt – and lost himself for just one liminal moment between memories. They drifted and faded with the tide, each pulse collecting sand, each wave exchanging foam, and he waited for her in the chilled mist watching the pomegranate sun recede, lazily, into its sea bed.

She'd be here soon.

If he hadn't fucked it up.

He pressed the coin into his palm like a worry stone, willing away thoughts of her stalking the streets of the City of Night, a galaxy of lights shooting stars against an empire of glass, and how the salt in her eyes would creep into their kiss – the taste shameful and foreign simply for being his.

There are worse things I've done.

His shoulders clenched tightly, cigarette nothing but a dying ember acting as a last excuse to draw breath. A montage of her face raged incessant before his eyes.

Her voice, it fell like honey, like a crest of woven love, but he said, "It isn't up to me," and he was sorry. He said he was sorry, but the words hung thin on the air. *Not yet,* he couldn't let go, and he felt her body morph to porcelain in his arms; he smelled their sweat on her skin and in her hair and he left her legs shaking but he couldn't keep it up; that morning he flew from the room.

Goddamnit, why'd you open your eyes? You weren't supposed to see me yet; I'll explain everything. I'd cut off my wings, I'd have stayed for you, he thought.

Just to see her face again.[61]

---

[61] Legs dangling from the bridge – it seems so high up here above an endless sea almost void of light – her arms and face were coated in a sea salt sheen, sealed in grime from the clouds of exhaust. She could see their beach from here, just steps from the pier where she found him swathed in silence atop the lowermost crag, ribs pushing out of his shirt as he hugged himself against the cold. Their beach where they held court over the sea and the city alike, sometimes talking until their voices cracked, sometimes saying nothing at all but making just enough noise for two. She saw the water losing ground every time it came ashore. *I know how you feel,* she whispered to the sea. She shifted her weight.

The metal beams beneath her shook with tension and moaned from the torrent of flashing lights careening past a dying sun that made her only bones shake.

That decayed sea smell of low tide mixed with gasoline.

She saw him standing close to the waves and sent him, in a whisper, the only prayer she could believe in, and then a blast of wind was in her ears upstaging the onslaught of shouts from above as she leapt, eyes open wide, into the cold water – four seconds was the longest wait – and became the precious China doll she loved without a heart.

He saw the ocean foam. The burning in his eyes was matched only by the ache in his heart.[62]

---

[62] Primo bozza [[canto]] in Italiano originale disponibile su richiesta.

The glass in this boudoir,
it was yours to twist and smile in
as you saw fit.
A torrent of tears and gaping anger caught inside the frame,[63]
each breathless scream of agony
or ecstasy
played back over the years.
Now only decay.
My face will freeze like yours, sometimes,
in the eyes and mouth,
just so, until I blush and smell your perfume
tinged in sweet smoke
as if the warmth of your breast and arms were all around me
and I were once again small enough to fit inside
the safety of your embrace.

Can it have been so long?

.7.1.13.

---

[63] Some days I am lost in time, a slave to its liminal dissonance. Plagued by echoes – or strengthened by them? – of those interred in memory.

Choke

Don't lose yourself to reverie, choking on your biggest regret[64]

You'll choke on that apple you were idly eating as he is summoned from the æther to bike past you, glistening in sweat as the bile rises in your throat in bitter memory of the taste, oblivious to your presence as you hope he'll stay; the only way to keep everyone safe.

Don't think about who you've lost by staying silent wading gently through moments feigning liminal retrogression.

Don't think about who you tried to protect.

[[*his name always priority over your own,*
and you've been told,
"This is why it happened to you."]]

Don't wonder if the cage they found was a curse you gave them; words fading in brief consequence, inconsequential[65]

You'll choke on the irony.

An interstitial exodus from all you wish to forget as your Ground Zero is the reflection of your eyes you know are dead and will remain as long as they dwell on the echoes of the past; reparation as you learn to breathe around restriction, releasing binds around hands, heart and throat, till you just choke.

Until you're rid of it, just choke.
Until it bleeds out clean, just choke.
Until purgation leaves you shaking, when there's nothing left but you, just choke.
Until the remnants of emptiness leave you calm in the quiet you have claimed, just choke.

---

[64] "Don't think of it as a mistake; things just happened to turn out this way."
[65] I can't say
I have no regrets today.

Until reflection gives no new wisdom from which to learn, to trace the steps leading you to exactly here, until you trust your own hand to clear the path, to reclaim each piece you gave away, you plucked out as soon as it offended him, just choke until each foreign shard he fed you is exhumed and his framing disillusions are just bad dreams, just ash between your teeth that you've stopped clenching, until it all comes out as bile, projected, hot and hissing on the ground,
get it out of you.

Until there's nothing left to vomit up, just choke.
Then breathe.
Then look deep into the eyes of your reflection.

And there you are.

You are only You, again.

Now: Never be that You, again.

Anyone tells you to swallow that bitter pill again, don't.
Don't you dare do it.
Just choke.

.25.4.14.

X's

Kiss to kill.
Eat to burst.
Dance to drop.[66]
Feel to burn.
Ache to live.

.27.4.14.

---

[66] Dance until your head stops; dance until your heart starts.

Baby Talk

There are pictures of you drooling into your grandfather's coffee as he engulfs your chubby almond cream hands in his – you grasp nothing but air, desperate as medicine – gnarled and wizened as tree trunks and with your dimpled wrists keeps time in the clanking of his watch, as he swears you love doing this, and sings, "Pound, pound pound on the taaaaaaaaaaaable!" as he waits for you to chime in.

There are pictures of him offering you a pumpkin cream cheese muffin you can't even pronounce as you shove the wrapper in its entirety into your mouth and drool bubbles in the crumbs.

There are pictures of you squealing nonsense into your bumble bee teething ring as the whole family looks on in Norman Rockwell tableau, three generations hanging on your every bauble and I wonder how you'll ever learn to really speak if no one ever says an articulate thing and will you gurgle and sing from your protruding fish belly to fill the absence of sound or will you drift, slowly and feral, into depleting radio silence?[67]

There are pictures of your grandmother shaking her hair to tickle your nose stuck scrunched — cheeks collapsing into one eye like all mass and matter into a precious black hole — you grunt in low tones in response as Grandpa chimes in, "You're such a happy baby," your brother barely two years older shaking his head at the whole scene until the grunting stops and your grandmother's head rears back and he states for the record staring down into his cookie in a monotone malaise,

"She pooped in your lap. And you smelled it."

And. Well.

No one took any pictures of your brother.

.11.7.14.

---

[67] I've seen your future. You have to be silent in order to be heard.

9/23

Buttons on a leather jacket.
The golden tint at the end of an Autumn day.
That subtle burn of your first sip of tea coating the twinge in your throat from sleeping through a cold night.
Tiny Asian women walking their tiny little dogs in their tiny yellow heels that match the tiny yellow bow in their hair and nothing else.
Waking up refreshed two hours before your alarm.
Motes of dust pirouetting between the trees.
Perfecting your lipstick in the reflection of a sword's edge.
That first drop of sweat down the side of your face.
When couples first close their eyes when leaning in for a kiss, trusting that their lover's lips will be there.
High tide.
When you see the yellow and blue sunsmudges on the side of things at the same time.
When friends affectionately tell you to go fuck yourself.
The sound of children laughing.
The colour of a puppy's tongue when it yawns.
Hugs lasting as long as they need to, with or without a silent plea.
Counting all the facets of colour in your skin.
Hearing, "It's better to have loved and lost," and knowing that love is never lost at all.
That snap when you know you caught the wind in the right curve of the sail.
Noses that wrinkle when they laugh.
When your leg won't stop shaking.
Fishtail braids.
Hightop socks and ankle boots.
Butterflies flitting in the morning glories.
When your focus narrows but gaze widens at the sweet spot of a fight.
The faint scent of lemon meringue, just for a second, wafting in the evening breeze.
Brevity.
Silhouettes in a dying sun.
Transitional lenses.
Multiverse theories.
When the knife hits the bull's eye.
A show you love and never finish.
Drinking something hot outside on a cold night.
Bright eyes encased in wrinkled faces.

Secret messages etched in stone.
The unshakable feeling someone's thinking about you.
The oil slick left by coloured lips swirling in the top of your glass.
Bright smiles hidden by bushy beards, like a secret, that always surprise you.
When bartenders know you don't want to see the bottom of your glass.
Seven-pointed stars tattooed on kneecaps.
The divot in your finger when you take off the ring.
When strangers tell you their life story: excited, vulnerable, completely trusting that your smile is theirs for as long as they need to speak.
When an old man waits for his precious little wife, two hands clasped on the wolf head of his cane, eyes fixed on the brief horizon of the street where he knows, if he's patient, she will inevitably be.
The swirling of milk into a fresh cup of Earl Grey.
That aching sound the binding makes when you open a book for the first time.
The smell.

.23.9.15.

2:47 – 9:23

It's 2:47 in the morning.

I'm unconvinced this is a good time for anything but I've slept already and the walls are gently whispering their intuitive silence so I know they're listening.

I hear the faint shudder of distant doors opening and closing.

I hear him turning over in bed with a sharp intake of breath to indicate he couldn't find me in his sleep to pull me close in a sheltering silhouette.

I hear that car finally drive off.

I hear him rub his eyes and face and roll over in sleepy resignation that it's probably for the best, whatever he's [[un/sub]]consciously decided.

I hear the air turn on. The fridge. The drip of the faucet. The scratching of this pen across the page. The heavy footsteps of a neighbour upstairs which worries me that this lumbering silence isn't completely my own but I'm not greedy and it's nice to know that someone, albeit unbeknownst to them, is enjoying it with me; that being said, Neighbour Person, I'm pretty sure you make tacos for a living.

And I have it on good authority that you should go the fuck to sleep.

I will judge you to your face.

Tomorrow.

[[In the *actual* tomorrow.]]

Politely, though.

I'll probably ask if you were doing ok, after hearing you pace till the floor is all but burger and trip a minimum of two times.

We may even find that you and I were having the same kind of night if we thought about it, formulating an innate sense of singularity in places we never thought to look.

But don't ask me what I was doing, awake, listening to you trip down the stairs, feeling the small of my back both shiver and sweat as I commit to consciousness and feel exhaustion settle into the space behind my eyes reserved for the after-image of spectral faces burned into the synapses keeping them connected to my skull, remaining just upright enough in this chair so as to stay the perfect amount of uncomfortable to not fall back asleep but not destroy my back.[68]

I was watering the cactus.

---

[68] Please just don't ask.

Yeah, that's it.

I was, uh. Returning videotapes.

I was destroying something beautiful and viddying some azure sky in deepest summer and any other excuse I can glean [[read: steal]] from media culture without getting caught and without inciting a follow-up question of any kind.

The point is, I'm awake.

I'm awake because there's a slight chill and I can feel the little hairs on my legs stand at attention though I shaved a day and ¾ ago.

I'm awake to hear the sounds of waning and waxing life in the hopes that if I'm patient I can reach into these rays of moonlight and mercury will have cascaded down and I can eat it.

Yes, I know what happens if I swallow mercury.

The point is:

I won't.

I never do. No matter how hard I try.

I'm awake because there's an Ingmar Bergman flick called <u>The Magician</u> that makes reality a construct of alcohol, well-placed storms and a fear of the Unknown. The problem is, none of that leads to actually cheating death, but it's a good movie anyway.

I'm awake because I dreamt he and I were traversing town in search of various things and found:

.a river.

.two men with a secret.

.a basement where the Joker didn't kill Superman in a Flash of retribution, but patiently waited while I interviewed Michael Keaton.

.the perfect crêpe.

.a building with unlocked doors where the security guard hi-jacked our elevator and rudely asked what we were doing there.

I'm awake because that's where I gave up.

I'm awake because, for once, that's where I woke up.

I'm awake because I can't remember a night without a nightmare which makes this night the exception which makes this night exceptional.

I'm awake because he deserves a night where I'm not thrashing awake or crying in my sleep.

I'm awake because the mind often reconstructs what it can't handle or doesn't understand into something familiar. This means that one thing you've been trying not to think about all day will be represented in your subconscious as some inherently unrecognizable trope, some painfully obvious obscurity, some series of malleable objects and phrases and projections of people making references that only you can understand while your mind and body recharge in this safe space that is a camera obscura inversion of reality to coax you into acceptance of whatever happens to be plaguing you in waking life.

I'm awake because the Holidays are a bad time for me. Which is shit. I love the Holidays and my family and him and his and friends and cooking till my eyes are liver oil and I'm awake because the period from Halloween to my birthday...

Well.

Words are slow. And, sometimes, chronicling them can become absolutely arbitrary.[69]

Maybe not today, and maybe not tomorrow, but soon and for the rest of your life.

I'm awake because last Winter is a period in my life that I want to forget. I've been through Summer and found that love could be calm, love could be peaceful, love could be kind. Autumn is flawless but my reflection within the decay became a distortion I couldn't forgive but I refuse to resent.

I'm awake because I want to recall Winter with deadened limbs and a numb cortex.

I'm awake because I'd take amnesia, because occasionally my nerve endings strain themselves up and out like lilies in a pond and I feel every whisper of my hair like stinging nettle across my back and my ribcage harbours a festering pool of napalm and that bile in your bones that flows freely when you're sick is all the time and I hate the sound of my goddamn name.

I'm awake because Winter haunts me.

I'm awake because I'm Haunted by memories I long to purge.

I'm awake because I remember the way Ghost called me Patricia – he insisted :: it was important to him :: on having a name for me that was only his – like a cracking whip, a hiss dripping with disdain with a smirk as I wince, to snap me to attention away from whatever beautiful sliver of myself I clung to, desperately, with shaking hands to remind myself, *This*

---

[69] So how about this –

:Writing Exercise:

Yesterday the boys were in the kitchen waxing philosophically about their dicks and where to hide them and Alan yells, "Patty. PATTY. Brian said, 'FRUITION.' That's right. My boy's got a college de*gree.*"

And I said, "I'm so proud of you, Bri. Your next word is 'calamitous.' Use 'calamitous' in a sentence."

[[calamitous because calamari :: calamari because Chuckie P :: Chuckie P. because "Guts." :: "Guts" because Haunted.]]

[[Saint Hapless strikes again. <3]]

ugliness is only temporary, but I don't remember the way he'd say he loved me.

I'm awake because this fact is the only one I can cling to securely. As if my mind has already tithed the dross of things that were never true.

Now I'm left with things that are.[70]

Now I wonder, "Why write this at all?"

The lady doth protest too much in retrospect, but during she was docile as a cow, whipped and branded with eyes closed and clenched jaw, blood filling in the cracks between teeth and lips and legs.

I'm awake because I want so desperately to be happy and held, encased in the Love that he cradles for me like a frightened bird with bruised wings and tiny, tinny lungs that forgot how to turn the wind into a home made of song.

When you live through something that leaves you broken you will do anything to keep the ones you love from experiencing the same.

I'm awake because I want to be nestled in the place he makes for me every night, my pillow the warm slope between his shoulder and chest – he's a side-sleeper now so he can have both arms around me – and, though he's ticklish, he doesn't mind when my hand rests on his right oblique, gently clenching and relaxing a liminal fist, like a child whose fingertips still need reassurance of security.

I'm awake because lately I haven't been able to stay in the place he makes for me before we fall asleep. Instead I toss and I turn and I dream of worlds where law is not iron but stainless steel and population is comprised of refugees who overdose on enzymes so the procedural replacement of limbs and organs and circulatory systems with adamantium and mercury and nanotech won't boil their brains; not that that'd be unfortunate for the Management, so much as inconvenient. The surgeons had no eyes or arms and what limbs they had on less than humanoid bodies were retractable and hypodermic machines programmed to enhance each corpus to the peak of its techno-physiological condition. Respectively, of course, to its species.

I spent a year and 47 days there either in the Pit or in the medical bunker. The objective was never to kill, though it happened; the pain was always more visceral than the absence in death just before another

---

[70] *It's about here where the self-awareness kicks in.*
Are you there, Margaret?
Jesus wept.

awakening on the table. The objective was to fight, mercilessly until it was over – in the Pit – and in Medica the objective was to stay alive long enough to enhance your tolerance for pain.

I'm awake because sometimes ancient forests bend and change, milky mid-morning light dancing off the whispering leaves but the ground moves as we hang from above, nestled in the branches, in graceful witness while we glide and the bark and the ground and the glistening reflections move as if someone's transitioning the aperture in our vantage point and refocusing in accordance with the mind; the Dark Man, who comes sometimes, hovers just out of frame, just present enough to destroy any sense of calm in this place and I know that he's infecting this, spreading silence, just silence, and the light is seeping away as if someone's turned the saturation down on my dreams and he isn't bigger but he's more and my scream is stolen from me so it becomes the whisper, a disturbance of breath merely shaking the leaves.

I'm awake because I was in a coffee shop and Ghost appeared looking haggard and desperate and I just wanted him to eat, to drink warm milk, to leave the bottle on the dresser but instigating the presence of care, even of Self, is an invitation of responsibility I can no longer accept and that's when I wake from that dream into another where he's broken in and standing over us in bed with the gun he took from his roommate's safe, just like he said he would, asking me who I'm sleeping next to and why did I leave and how he's grown to hate me but I wasn't supposed to leave and the sound as he squeezes the trigger turns into me screaming but I'm really awake now and the panic distorts my sight and steals my breath and my heart screams as if the bullet were a molten rock nestled in my chest with no exit wound and his name is laser printed on the outer curve of my third rib. Like an Enochian curse from which I will never be clean.

But then I'm awake. And he's still sleeping next to me. This fallen angel from a Botticelli, perfectly imperfect and dreaming his own dreams.

I'm awake because he is the dream that kisses every scar on my heart and in the mornings he lifts me so I can feel weightless, so I can forget the shackles I left from a phantom looking for the blood of a restless heart to consume, to remember what it is to be living a life that is human and the concept they believe to know as "love."

That's his alarm.
I am Jack's mental fondue.

He says when his alarm goes off and I'm dead asleep the first thing I do is pull him closer and *mmmmmmph* in disapproval of the sound.

We argue on days when he leaves for work before I do and I wake to find him gone without kissing me goodbye and I'm winning until he regales me with the conversation we had while I slept, what languages I spoke to tell him – he thinks – that I love him and how many times I kissed him and where as I nestle deeper into his neck, the albatross weighing him down to the bed, oblivious as to how much he needs to leave for work; he's winning until I say, "I remember none of this," and smile.

Relieved anyone could see past the ugliness I carry inside. No matter how much more is left to tell him, yet I know how hard it is for him to listen when I speak.

He fought with his jacket in the foyer the way he makes fun of me for. I told him, *See? Karma,* and he said that he regrets nothing; whatever he did was obviously amazing because he gets to come home to me every night. I said, because I've been writing this, *What if I'm your punishment and you're my salvation?*

He said, because I've been writing this, *I know what you're doing and why; just think of me and know I love you and try to have some fun today. And kiss me one more time.*

Always already one more time.

I'm awake because I need to give these words to you.[71]

I'm awake because my life will be spent finding every piece of myself I've kept hidden away and feeding them to you, one by one, like pomegranate seeds so I can suck the juice from your lips, red as Jokanaan's, and finally find absolution.

---

[71] And trust me, I know how difficult my words can be sometimes, but I need you to stay with me as I write them, as they unfold, as they form on the page because as long as I keep writing my narrative will continue to change. And I am happier than I've been but I can't stay here and these words need to be bled out of me so that I can see where I once laid myself interred through the aria of my liminal death.

I don't know you yet but my words will one day touch you and I need you to tell me how. I need you like the tide needs the wake; always a pull and then a push and we are both, in turn.

I need you like the Ocean needs the Moon.

I love you the way the Moon caresses the waves of the Sea in the early morning where their whispers are the only sound that's heard. If we were the Moon and the Sea we'd make love in the crashing of each diurnal tide unleashing a power kept nestled deep beneath'e waves.

I love you the way the Moon loves the Sun, as violently unyielding as a force of nature with enough time to kill as a few spaces between stars. If we were the Sun and the Moon then we'd make love using nothing but the tips of our fingers splayed out in rays of light and the soles of our feet kneading softly on the shore.

I'm awake because no sunrise should be spent alone which is why you're here with me and whomever you are, I already love you as I love the supple thickness of this script flowing freely onto this page. I love you as the magic of something empty becoming full – of words, caresses, love – and what you've done for my heart and mind. I love you as selfishly as I love how I feel because of you because love is a selfish child willing to do anything to make what they love feel loved so they can keep feeling loved.[72]

I'm awake because we'll only have forever and that's not long at all, not long enough for the love you will have unleashed within me.

I'm awake because when you have so many truths without understanding they can't be facts so they become a mythology. In life we become siphons of knowledge transferring facts between places in our psyches from greater to lesser thus obtaining an equilibrium we refer to as Wisdom.

The fact is that I am loved by a loving, compassionate man.

A truth is that I was lead to believe this was more than I could ever deserve and the flashes of photo negatives will haunt me until I bleed out the miasma still flowing within me.

The fact is my tolerance is superhuman yet I am still in pain.

These truths pertain to why.

I'm awake because the apartment rested on stilts of moonlight held high above the god particle as eons of stars drift past the walls of mirror and each planet let their moons become gods so I could see them holding my buttresses in place as korai in the colonnade of this, my very own celestial temple. I sip my tea in the resplendence that is this immortal quiet in an oasis of space. I watch them through the glass. Breathing in the silence of the darkness briefly interrupted by the glimmer of stars reflecting off their humanoid faces gently turning, taking in the wonder that is perception shifted from ephemeral to corporeal self. Each pillar

---

[72] Let's make love like children.
Let's make love like tea leaves in boiled water.
Let's make love like milk and honey.
Let's make love like fingers on taut strings and keys; like lips on the mouthpiece of flutes.
Let's make love like sunlight in a brook babbling softly down a hidden waterfall.
I'll never feel my eyelashes fluttering against my own cheek; you can.
I love you like that.
Try it. It's impossible.
That's why I need you.
That's why you need me.
I need you like I need to write these words and you need to read them.
When you're gone I miss you like the stained glass in a rose window misses the waves.

connecting floor with ceiling fluted deeply; the acanthus hung in high relief. From here I could see the edge of darkness illuminated in the wake of every star and though I stood chiaroscuro, hip resting against the marble island greeting living room with kitchen, as the focal point in my own Universe, transcending any boundary, my only thought remained that I was grateful to be alone.

Finally tasting grim leaves at the knell of my tea cup I retreated for a bath.

My hall was lined in the portraiture of statuary with an exaggerated patina providing value in the wake of each downturned eye, the folds of wet drapery more sensual than the feminine forms they clung to leading to a perfectly circular door. The water flowed and sang, my silk robe kissing my shoulders and neck as it fell to the floor and I watched the tendons in my hips and back twist and extend in the mirror, reacquainting myself with my Self and wondering where I'd been all this time.

Settling in, I felt the heat cleansing every pore in my skin as the salt melted to soothe me, idly using the water to wash soap scum off the marble base as the scent of lavender and frankincense filled the room and nestled gently beneath the blanket of perfumed water.

A chill shimmered up my pinking skin.

I turned my head to see him and time stopped.

His slender frame filled the doorway with a pressured presence of dissent, embarrassment and well-informed yet feigned confusion as the bottle hung limp at his side, having freely given itself to his will. And my lavender became tainted with cigarettes; my frankincense seeped in rum.

Holding himself together he mumbled a quick aside in the form of snide apologies for interrupting me in such a sensual vulnerability in a way we both knew from his eyes wasn't apologetic at all as he always had such a dizzying way with words where the tonality one might affect to illustrate scathing ridicule he'd mimic when conveying *innocent banter*. This led him to stumble which caused the bottle to sway, accentuating the wild gesticulations that followed each slurred insult and brackish accusation reflected in the vanity to his right. Flashes of guilt schloshed out the bottle resting in little pools in the bottom of the mirror that gave him pause for a few precious seconds before continuing on his vein as he leveraged – so often he leveraged his vein – each step creeping closer to the bath brought vapours of noxious anxiety ebbing on the edges of steam serving as my protective nimbus.

Insults bordered accusations.

Accusations became threats.

Threats led to his hands coming dangerously close to the walls of my tub and the nimbus of steam seemed to burst as his words reverberated in the same decibel as that of an echo captured inside a bell jar. I heard him now in perfect clarity, recognizing, finally, the frequency in which I had struggled to stay in order to match him remained a wailing siren and I never fully heard him before. I saw him now for who he was. Remembered every word that should have been enough.

I took a breath as I stood and as I shook the anger rose through me like a flame up an oiled lattice and when I took his eyes he receded as one might in the realization that their harsh words are purely a rehearsed fiction to transfer pain.

This time, quietly, he begged me to reconsider. He found me here and that meant he was a part of me and he apologized, eyes clouding with tears, and he wanted me back but he didn't want to hurt me anymore but he couldn't trust himself and asked me to please remember what we had...

I took a breath to reclaim agency.

He threw the bottle.

It always happened this quickly, I thought, watching the location of every shard ricochet and fall, committing them to memory so I'd know where to stop him if he turned to pick them up, as I'd learned even the jagged edge of a broken hanger could be used on his right arm if I argued with him.

He reared back yelling. He knew what we had and it was nothing. I was a liar and untrustworthy and ruined his life and he needed therapy and medication because of me and it was my responsibility because he needed neither when I was near him and he needed my help and he hated me and she meant nothing and I wasn't supposed to leave.

And for once I spoke without fear for his safety or psychological recoil that this, both his fear and broken vanity, was the reason I left. Not cold feet, not someone else, but the guilt-blame vortex pummelling my mind and soul when he drank, when we fought, when I couldn't get close. And I know now that it wasn't his fault. And I know now what he's endured, what he's been through to become this way, what he tried for a lifetime to be anything but without the clarity of context to prove each fragile fear he had no choice but to be disproven in his own mind, losing ground against the black hole of his past swallowing the heart of his star. I loved him, who I thought him to be, so fiercely I blamed distance for miscommunication, I became patient with despair, and as I clutched his hand to prevent him from drowning I slowly slid into morbid complacency contradicting every monolith I'd erected in my psyche to remind me just how far I'd come and let the affluence of borrowed dissent betray me in the hopes I could find the epicentre of his darkness and breathe light into the cracks in the hopes I might ever feel loved instead of coveted, but.

Love does not infect the heart to kill it.

Love does not extinguish light through distortions of beauty.

Love is not an invasion of trust, a chemical stripping of autonomy.

Love does not remind someone of all the ways in which they are unworthy.

Love is not fucking physical manifestations of hate and blaming who you love for the moment of weakness.

Love does not come in waves of degradation and convenient dementia.

Love is not explosions raging incessant when they reach out to their friends in moments of distress, reminding them you've talked to all of their friends already so they needn't bother trying to contradict you.

Love does not force them to watch self harm though a camera lens crying, "You made me this way," into your middle and thumb.

Love is not what we had.

Love is what I wanted us to be.

The love we had was the kind not meant to last and I'm learning, now, the signs we ignored in the hopes of avoiding any sort of life without Love.

Truth is he blamed his psychoses on a woman before and I believed him until I saw how much he needed her.

Truth is I hated her for what he swore she did to him but now all I feel for her is sorry.

Truth is lashing out irrationally is a form of guilt when you don't know where your emotions come from and they begin to betray you.

Truth is I got tested when I found out he didn't use a condom because of all the needles and dicks he swore she hid inside herself in her grief of missing him in the short period that he was mine and there were needles behind my eyes penetrating my perception infecting synapses in my brain with borrowed poison sticking to my spine and I drank every day when I found out to dull the buzzing and reminded myself we weren't finished and you forgive people when you love them and I spent hours in the gym destroying every sinew and stopped eating because my gut was noxious waste and when he saw my fragile bones screaming out of my hips he kissed them and told me how beautiful I had become and when he'd find me gently staring out from the prison in my head he'd leave teeth marks on my inner thighs to wake me and swore he didn't mind, swore it was better for him when I was dry.

My body desperate to tell me what my heart refused to accept.

Truth is.

Truth is, he could never love me as every word of love was borrowed. It wasn't his fault; he didn't lie and he didn't hurt me following the footsteps of the man he hated but he didn't know what the truth was and everything progressed so fast in the passion of what we believed to be a pinnacle of cinematic mastery but I didn't know how to brave those depths from such a distance and though I tried to help I botched every cue because at the center was a seed that I took with me:

I was a 13 month rebound in love with a man too in love with another woman to admit he didn't hate her.

"So go be with her," I said, *this is still a dream, darling,* stepping out of the lukewarm water, slowly backing him out of the room with my countenance, "and please understand why I can't be there to help you anymore."

There's no room anymore in my heart or my head for him as both will be exhumed and purged until every trace is cleansed and cauterized. Dark memories will be replaced with love and loveliness and beauty and he can have his <u>Weekender</u> of long shots drifting and lilting piano keys because there will be angels in my life emulating humanity to fulfill Desire and I will never have a spotless mind free of this.

No.

But I would give him the damnatio memoriæ the way he gave me.

I'm awake because the birds are awake. I'm awake because they are singing. The bat in my ceiling has finally fallen back to sleep.

I'm awake because I moved past him in my celestial bathroom, trusting he'd be gone by the time I got back, and took a Bogart trench coat from the closet like a Revolutionary as I opened the glass held closed by my korai. I took a breath gazing down upon an infinite precipice and a white light filled me as I let myself step off the edge and fall through the gaseous space between stars, splitting my teeth against the pressure of propulsion as I exploded past, flayed by the heat of distant suns tearing off my skin in strips and the meat exposed beneath was cleansed in flames that held my nimbus close to me as the earth rose beneath. I landed deep within a pit that I created as the dregs of fallout from my meteor pierced the ground and I could see the manifestations of miasma that I took with me, that I always carry with me, scattered in the pit before it could scab. I had almost… I had almost forgotten how to use my legs, but I climbed out, muscles screaming in battery acid, found the ground beneath my feet and walked.

Out.

Away.

I just walked until my eyes receded back into my skull and the pressure forcing my teeth out of their cradles was nothing but a dull ache reminding me to breathe. I walked until my lungs were merely there to draw breath, my legs extensions of my will to continue moving and my brain another muscle that I used to forego anonymity. To fragment focused innovation in favour of stark objectivity. But no matter how far I walked the ground reminded me it didn't care and I still did and the road in this dream will not end until I let it.

I conjured a taxi to take me to town and once there I counted every steel beam rusted and bent to slow my breath, every lamp light that blew out as I walked by. The sounds of the street invaded my reverie and gave it resistance which made it mine. In reclamation I ducked into a café and ate enough eggs and cheese and peppers and raspberry pastry to settle my brain inside my stomach and let it stay there. The apartment I kept on the ground was at the end of the block and I thought about another coffee but realized I couldn't keep putting this scene off until later. I paid my bill and my projections gazed at me wondering whether I knew I was giving penance for something I provided. *I didn't. Now I do.*

The door was unlocked, of course, and my family bustled in the low light of my kitchen and living room. Boxes and bookshelves and unstrung guitars and the music playing was what my mother wanted me to hear and when I saw her face I faltered because she was the closest to knowing what I'd been keeping from them all this time so I looked to see my father's shoulders bent to pack another load of my things into the truck to take me back. To take me home. *But home is nowhere.* I walked forward aware of the dirt and blood and sweat caked into the fabric of my trench coat to hug my father but before I got to him I heard my mother say, "Well. Time to put your life back together like last time. And the time before that. And the time before that."

There was a throw pillow on the floor unclaimed by boxes. My legs stopped pulling me forward and when I collapsed to it every ache in my bones I'd held back from screaming came streaming out from my eyes into the pattern of this tremulous scene in wailing, gasping breaths I heaved in reparation for my soul I hemorrhaged onto the stone floor.

I am awake and these dreams are what keep me from forgetting who I am.

These dreams hold clues and traces of my Self that I tried to let go of for the sake of someone else and in order to reclaim them, I need to understand how they were lost. I need to know what of me is worth reclaiming.

These dreams remind me not to fall prey because I find the ones struggling and sick on the fringes of the pack and offer my neck as comfort so that they can feel powerful but inevitably they realize that power scares them and I become the immediate representation of the dominance they covet and fear. As if they believe strength to be something forbidden, something only to exist in a fantasy, and because I don't believe in the fantasy it is merely a character that I play.[73]

These dreams are the mirror in which I see myself offering my only bones to those I love to set what someone else has broken without hope of return, and as the mirror shifts and bends through temporal space I see the way my eyes and body have shifted in the wake of a time when I was once whole but now I am a broken summary of parts lately laid, incomplete and unrecognizable to my Self.

These dreams remind me of what I've done. What harm I have caused trying to help those whose troubles I didn't fully understand, enabling them to use me as a tuning fork to recalibrate who they could be if the darkness didn't feel so deep, thinking love could soothe their aching bones the way it did mine, always resonating within the realm of their frequency as mine we never seemed to find time for, giving salves unmatched by the ailments I only saw through a screen leaving them as broken as they were before but now exposed and the cost is the weight I bear.

I'm awake because I chose every path that led me to this moment and as much as I know I need to bleed this out of me, there's a voice just screaming that I have no right to; reminding me that there's an explanation for every pain that I've endured and them being the cause doesn't mean that they're at fault because we all suffer incomparable hurts and will never heal in the same way and the shrapnel that infects me from exposure to their pain only penetrated so deeply because I opened myself to house the theatre of their inner war believing I'd be strong enough to withstand the fallout until they found catharsis. My decisions, my words, my hands and my silence brought me to exactly here. I am still in pain because I need to crawl back inside of these moments that haunt me in order to better understand them so that I no longer cower from them in shame.

The fact is that I am still in pain and I'm awake because sometimes I am afraid to sleep and these truths pertain to Why but I wait in fragile recompense for reality to finally be sweeter than any dream I could conjure up.

[[.*redacted*.]]

My hope is that the next time I am lifted I won't be afraid to fall. But I know who I am. And why, a little more completely, now. And I know how difficult it is to meet my eyes in the mirror without wincing, so that hope is more of a serenity prayer I repeat when I can't stop shaking. I'm awake because the guilt is a blanket given to me, pocked with disease that is worming inside of me through the scratches from the harsh fabric

---

[73] Mein Herr, I am not worthy to receive you, but only correct me as to who I am and I shall be healed.

rubbing but I don't trust my body not to freeze without its borrowed warmth and that fear enables each borrowed infection to fester as I ache with how much I fought to get as far as I had come before another love brought me to my knees. I keep neglecting me.

I'm awake.

I'm awake because deep within me there is a seed. And no matter how hard it is to breathe I keep watering that seed and whispering to it that if it is hungry it should feed on that pain and the scars that I carry so that when it grows I won't know because I'll have forgotten what this pain feels like as the space it occupied will be filled with pure creation taking root within the marrow of my only bones to find room and I'll have found a reflection of the love that I possess that I'm not afraid to share and, whomever you are, I'll know you when you speak and I'll seep into your skin like spring water that shed its form, but it is your heart I will crawl into, safely encased within the grotto of your bones that remain your own and you won't need mine to soothe you and the love that has filled me will bloom into you with a fragrance that gives you light and I can sleep and I can dream in a peace uninterrupted until each bone I've stolen back to me can set and knit and heal until I remember what it is to feel whole and when you breathe deeply in the warmth of our Love it will be me that fills you.

The way this seed will fill me.

I'm awake.[74]

.17.12.14.
9:23am[75]

---

[74] *It was a half bad dream that was way too long, my whole life, it seemed. Then someone started digging me up; turned my headstone into dust.*
    Alkaline Trio

[75] The world never ends when it's supposed to.
21.12.14.

The Little Things

On my way to Pourhouse Café an older gentleman in a pea coat and Dr. Who scarf said, I originally thought to the æther, "Don't worry so much sweetie; you're a genius."

I almost missed it as the cadence of my footsteps kept time with the falling snow, as I followed a path of broken brick beneath my feet that only I could see. Delayed synapses connected, I finally looked up at him, quizzically, uncertain how long he had been paying attention, wondering if the Inklings were still in session, worrying how much he could really see.

"I'm a professor here," he says in validation, perceiving my unease as his responsibility somehow, "and only geniuses look like that."

"I'm not a genius, sir, but thank you," I said, snailing back inside myself. "I'm a nightmare."

And I think what I meant to say was, half in apology, half in appreciation for the sudden kindness extended, *I'm just currently entrenched in thought about this nightmare I had last night,* but my brain works much faster than my voice can keep up and sometimes what I mean to convey and what I actually express are seldom comparable and the gentleness of strangers interrupting ugly thoughts creates a dissonance within me not easily resolved and though I meant to reciprocate kindness I can't remember restful sleep and I may or may not believe myself to be *the* nightmare.

And I think, sometimes, when I'm paying for my right to live with nothing but an envelope at the corner of this busy street, that words are the only things on which I continuously depend. Which means, as you can guess, they betray me more than anything else could[76] in the fact that what I mean to say and what I mean aren't always the same because I will always try to protect you from the miasma that I carry but the words work for me always expressing what I mean before I realize that I do when I'm not careful.

And it doesn't happen often but if you're paying attention you'll see that we're both just as surprised by what I said and I always apologize with my eyes because if you are paying attention it's always at least a little unfortunate.

Which is how I generally know that I've neglected some things[77] when the words that should come from me end up putting me in place.

---

[76] This isn't tragedy. My words are the vehicle through which I traverse my mind and they never disappoint, even when I'm disappointing.

[77] Not entirely, you understand; it's more like a hair that's split but had enough protein to keep growing until it split again and you pull at the end to get rid of the evidence — as if anyone would ever be looking

What I mean to say is, I'm sorry you're sleep deprived and probably having a bad day because you laid awake with me to tell me beautiful things as I fought with my eyes to be lidless, as I laid there trying to be held and I walked away from the gentleman fighting not to blink because the sound of the shutter dropping brings a montage of nightmare filling my vision all the way from my lids cracking from disuse to my lashes stiff with salt as I try, hours later, to reconstruct every beautiful thing you told me to think about instead so I didn't have to speak.[78]

.2.1.15.

---

[78] Fuck. Did I mail that check or recycle it? Some subhuman chudling is about to have a great day at my expense and Jesus Christ, if that doesn't explain my entire life, currently...

We perpetuate loneliness with behaviour that ensures we are alone.[79]

.16.1.17.

---

[79] What action, if any, occurs without a neurological genesis?
Psychoses as the result of some disorder in situ within the brain's response patterns.
Minor offenses: slips of the tongue/pen :result as well as building blocks; the breadcrumbs we would follow to a proper diagnosis, so to speak. Natural medicine – as psychology could be considered metaphysical – leaves no small quirk or tick, even hiccough, to chance as being unrelated: so, too, would one proceed in this case to take all whim or fancy to heart to be documented.
However, without proper guidance to understanding this may lead to panic and [[psychic/cyc]]lical hypochondria.
Without foundation, stable footing, any step forward is suspect of hindrance; broken bones improperly set healing at the expense of bones and tissue surrounding in a gradual distortion of viable function to be inevitably and inappropriately attributed outwardly, consistently at risk of reeling against those closest to you.

> *A squirming mind hurts*
> *those who would seek contentment.*
> *Let miasma fade.*
>
> *.:.*
> *I see no power*
> *O'ertake me but that which*
> *I create for myself.*
>
> *.:.*
> *Distractions willing,*
> *I will never see myself.*
> *I will be focused.*

.23.9.10.

Take Back This Tulpa; Let Me Sleep

Depression isn't permanent.
There are moments of lucidity.
There are moments* :: people :: landscapes :: days :: nights :: fuzzy faces
that make you laugh :: smile :: cry :: snuggle + fall asleep happy.

[[As opposed to happily.]]

Intelligence is difficult.
Sometimes the acuity of one's intelligence is directly proportional to the
effic[[ien/a]]cy of one's emotional recall, and[80] sometimes completely
innocuous moments* remind you of *that* moment :: person :: place;
that one time
that's either resolved or isn't or still hurts or doesn't
but you remember how it felt
even when you're remembering how happy you are.

Love is a death of ego and is therefore the one thing we fight against most.

If you've known a home then you know what love should be and often
never is; often we'll just keep our silence to ourselves for the sake of
appearances.
As in, ours.[81]
As in, we edit our selves for the sake of the eyes that look at us for the sake
of them never looking back differently than we want but representing
yourself is hard when you don't know who you are or who you've been
with[82] because we can only know others as deeply as we know ourselves.

---

[80] hopefully I'm lying but I know that I'm not
[81] Early mornings
all you hear is the occasional sound
of a car
the whispering of shadows and
the wind
patiently waiting to end
so it can begin

[82] who you've aligned your life and choices with, whose energy you've consistently tried to
match, with whom you've inadvertently molded your own to find each piece given to them
was ravenously consumed but reciprocity was never a concept they intended to swallow and
they demand you rely on them, demand they take care of you but you know they can't, not
with what they're going through, so you care for both, hoping it's enough to soothe them, and
you'll be able to just love in peace.

And you can't blame them for not wanting this because you don't even want this but you wish they could just let it fade and let you stay quiet when you need to when you know it's always better that way in the end.

The point is, I don't call people I can't lie to that I'll be ok when every muscle in my body has atrophied and is leaking, just, seeping outta me save for each tender ventricle, aching from overuse, terrified of disuse, in an otherwise obedient machine it remains the one cog over which I have no control, and I have no bones, only salt pillars making my insides ache while my heart is on fire and I can't use my voice without it breaking.

Not that you'd know.

The only ones that do know when not to bring it up. Cause that's another form of love I need. Almost as often as any other.

.28.9.15.

Good Girl

Innocence is fickle and I don't come when called.

My Mother dreamt I gave it up,
discarded it like an unused toy,
and I don't have the heart to correct her.
Better to believe I never wanted it. ~~Better to believe I made that choice.~~
But the choice I made I didn't understand
and that's why I'm here now.
~~That's who I am now.~~
Discarding any semblance of sweetness or fragrant truth.
~~but some truths are easier than others.~~
The thing about trauma* is it's always veiled and it always comes from
someone.
~~Words appearing wreathed in smoke.~~
And the ties to that someone needle into your skin
and twist
and writhe
until they're nothing but knots
and you could cut them
burn the evidence
cauterize the wound til it's nothing but a scar
but I don't heal that way.
~~I don't feel that way.~~
I knead them like sinews,
unravel each knot so when I'm ready to discard them
~~I've understood their purpose inside me.~~

I let go without consequence.
I've let go that it's Providence;
my Mother would disagree.
but I've tithed the dross of things that aren't true
now I'm left with things that are.
~~I'm left with Truths that scar.~~[83]

.27.3.17.

[83] Me: Beneficence is unconditional. I don't view it as a weakness, but... I do feel weak, from time, because of it.

Them: You're too much for people because you haven't done your part; you choose to be this way.

Trauma* is the irrational fear that an experience you had once may happen again, no matter how much evidence you've acquired to objectively prove otherwise.

It's a pain: a weakness in your joints that occurs with a memory exuding anger, panic, duress that halts the passage of time to splice every relative moment orbiting its epicenter into the growing pastiche of who you fear you'll always be; who you never want to be again.

It's an ugliness: a faerie's imprint in your cheek through which you dig and dig and gouge at hoping to be rid of it yet never digging deep enough to scrape away the scar tissue. In the end, it's your savagery against yourself that will be your own undoing.

The love you mistakenly ignored struggling to define what it is you truly hate.[84]

.23.2.17.

---

[84] tl;dr -

Sometimes irrationality is as simple as never wanting to say, "Yes," again for fear of an outcome that could never possibly be.

Golem

Me: I hyperbolize the hilarity of small, delicate, innocent tropes so as not to normalize the gravity of trauma and the weight that continuously plagues me in waking life which, I've learned from extensive conditioning, serves merely to provide discomfort[85] in social situations. I just want to smile; to laugh. I just want peace and forget, for a few moments, the weight that I carry and the way, I am told, I should feel.

Them: Jesus, she's attention seeking and loud.

---

[85] Why do they call it
post-partum depression
& not
mourning sickness?

Recall

If sleep is the descent
into neutrality
- our mental ground zero -
we become

d i s c   o   n   n   e   c t e d

from our holds in this world.
Give ourselves away.[86]

how

how does one resolve
emotional fatigue[87]
in favour of contentment?

Thriving on
moments b[[u/o]]rrowed.
Transcribing a moral transcendence
from just above
pandæmonium.

I have barely healed from the fall
&the mark is hot upon my brow.

I close my eyes
not from pain
but from the d[[e/i]]spærate wish
to withhold these images
from memory.

.12.3.17.

---

[86] Feeling cognitively discordant
with a faint suspicion that
this is the way I should have been feeling
for quite some time;

[87] The afterbirth of emotional labour for which I willingly volunteered

Morningstar

Puncture what I know as Truth as the final bastion,
in reverence, in sacral abandon;
who could I betray in situ?
who would watch me drop the veil?

as patiently as a sentient citadel
in quiet resignation of fated happenstance –
to do so would be to betray my very self interred within my own
reflection,
locked beyond my present understanding
of who I could have been all this time
yet finally understanding
why it has taken this long to truly be so.
Who I may have become is of absolutely no consequence.
I had no option but to be precisely as I am now,
bound by my own limitless potential
to a rock of my own design.[88]

How many livers can I borrow simply to be capable of giving another?

I could light the world ablaze
yet the fire in him
is the only flame I find worth stealing
if only to recreate the divine epiphany
that dwells within those eyes.

Oh to truly be a god.

.2.11.17.

---

[88] May I have residence here?

INVENIES

Fermentation:
their child will putrefy,
reborn as a Peacock's Tail

ii.

Such transience in the dead of night; such luck we'll never know.
What follows is a killing joke. No patience for the fold.

Nolita

You are my every influence within this quick Nolita morning; a faded rose sky turns my fingertips into crystal caverns that cradle warmth into a secret I can hold in my hand.

Such Wilde fantasies I possess of trapping imperfections within a matted glosse finish, the fat over lean, my canvas is heavy dripping inner monologues into a bell whose song is a nightingale sunrise.

I leave Art in my Mirror, not my Faith, something malleable and easily forgotten within an acrylic cage, no sins carved into sunken cheeks and eyes disappearing through grief, cringed and imprinted behind aching eyelids.

No prayers to parch my lips, un-blushed yet aubergine.

The blood will flow within my veins as oil, heavy and glistening with the faintest smell of turpentine to subdue you absinthine with a kiss, warm and sweet.

Wet as decay.[89]

.24.4.12.

---

[89] Sanctify reality through transubstantiation of the self; apotheosis occurring once we leave our pandæmonium behind. Kill your Self existing solely in the putrefaction.

Eat it.

Fucking eat it.

At the birth of a new Monday, just past midnight, the wind whispers at my window a vacant lover I can't decide if I should let in.

What spectres dance at the edge of Oblivion?[90]

.30.10.12.

---

[90] My heart races and yet I only wish to be still.

Savage Defiant

"But I don't want comfort. I want God. I want poetry, I want real danger, I want freedom, I want goodness; I want sin."
"In fact," said Mustapha Mond, "you're claiming the right to be unhappy."
"Alright then," said the Savage defiantly, "I'm claiming the right to be unhappy."

Aldous Huxley, <u>Brave New World</u>

I want poetry. I want real danger. I want freedom. I want goodness. I want sin.

I want heartache and a painful love. I want harsh winters. I want scars – broken teeth and bones. I want sunrises that melt the dead icelands and give them rebirth. I want hunger. I want my cheeks to sink and my hips to be hooks from which my jeans seem to hang and my shoulders to scream out like bird bones. I want to be out of my mind – frenziac, astral, wild in epiphany. I want to make love till I'm blind and my body swells and my arms are stretched wide and I can finally see without my body, feel without my eyes. I want passion. I want pandæmonium. I want to experience Heaven, ~~even~~ especially if I have to fall. I want to feel what the Accuser felt, to be cast from the presence of infallible and limitless grace and to know, truly, the consuming emptiness of Hell.

I want to claim what I have, by all rights, inherited.

I want to earn my Hell[91] by the savagery with which I've lived.

.7.3.13.

---

[91] *And the sirens' call began to ring louder. And the wind picked up and the crags loomed on before us, the end of the earth approaching our secret solace with its endless storm hiding beyond the steel clouds trembling in their darkness. And we'd go wandering in the halls. We'd drift closer to what we knew would become the Center...*

[[Excerpt from Zeit(f: Phœnix Wings:: Exuent)]]

To hear a name is to know what
people call you.
To know your name is to acknowledge
the essence of you; as wyrd[92] as I am,
I have impeccable timing for enlightenment.

.15.3.14.

---

[92] One sees what one sees and one knows what one knows.
But it doesn't pay to talk about it. Apparently.

Something Borrowed;[93] Something New

The Sun lead Day after Day into Life - *no direction but what the compass said was East* - in a trudging chorus of resolution. There was a time he would have painted the sky for anyone watching, kissed the water in passionate bursts and caressed every petal just to taste the silk nectar but he grew tired of the beauty below. The aching perfection of the world stifled him. He hid his face behind the clouds and the mountains and let the
rain rain rain r a i n d o w n rainbows
and lingered longer and longer behind the horizon, retreating earlier, letting the dreariness recede; he was sick of the bleak brilliance of each dim lit Day betraying his reflection till he hid his face behind the Sea letting the heavens drift without him and as the waves rose and fell in the deafening silence around him, he fell asleep.

Sick in apathy.

He dreamt of storms ravaging the mountains that were his shelter, lightning penetrating the Earth to its core and the gaping maw spread wide enough to swallow him and the pressure was pulling him in to be buried.

When he awoke, he was afraid –
his sin washed over him as the tide changed from high to low and he rushed to the crest of the waves to bring Day back as he swore he would, as he swore himself, as he swore to his duty anew in unfaltering fervour at the horror of his hubris but before he reached the break, he
stopped.

The Sea and its skies were illuminated.

But how? He had slept...

He had slept and Day never managed to change without him before but here he is faded in the crest of a light so mesmerizing it pained him. It was a light without his care; a darker but warmer light that glistened in the

---

[93] For a time, I'd spend night after night drinking in the stars,
sharing each transformed constellation
with anyone who didn't know any better,
reflecting on what the stories could be,
burning and pregnant with a mythology of my own
not yet realized.

waves the way his light never could and he was angry for wishing to bathe in that light, ashamed that the waves could seem happy without him.

Then he saw her.

The light that the waves, though she let them borrow the stars, wished only to embrace as they pulled harder and harder from the shore. The light that left a quiet over the chaos and let it breathe.

The endless light was Moon and Sun trembled for her.

He crept slowly, beneath the waves, back to Day, intoxicated with the memory of her imperfect yet soothing glow.

He needed her light.

Sun came back, again and again, beneath the waves, every time he stayed longer
and longer
longer than he should
letting darkness fall sooner
letting her night linger
in the hopes she would know she would see that he favoured her light and if she wanted he would give her the sky just to watch her move and paint in vibrant mythology the story of her eyes and let him watch but something was wrong – she seemed... less. She began to seem less as each night wore on and the beauty she once held for him had faded into her sadness and she'd come to caress the waves but little by little she began to hide her face.

He couldn't stand it. He wished to hold her, embrace her very self and let her borrow his light if need be, though he felt his light too harsh to compare.

He began to chase the night to ask her, comfort her, anything, anything to see more than the sliver of her beauty she left behind in the sober light of mo(u)rning.

Each night he'd chase her and each night she'd turn her face;
he begged Venus for help and she laughed.

He began to burn the waves at every chance because they always seemed to be reaching for her but every night she cooled them in a kiss that cradled their depth.

In blind jealousy he asked Orion to shatter Morningstar who followed her too close
but Moon picked up every piece, careful as god, and scattered them in the Sea.

He watched the glimmering shards drift and fade and in his anger the heat became a syphon out of which he seemed to seep
and when he looked up, once again,

his was the only light he could see.[94]

And Moon turned her face.

.17.4.14.

---

[94] Once upon a time, a girl told this story to a boy she loved. She twisted every word in petals behind her lips before filling the pages she ached for him to read, but she gushed aloud before reading the words, spilling every detail like the shards of Morningstar drifting in the Sea and when she finally stopped, she, she didn't... know.
The boy was furious. What she wrote for beauty he took as accusation, that Moon felt Sun wasn't good enough for her. And she didn't know it could mean that and it was the first time she realized she could ever be someone's Moon and she didn't mean that but
the boy yelled and
the girl cried and
the pages curled black as the words burned and drifted deep into the cavernous oubliette that Lot 90 inevitably birthed within a chasmic foundation of strictly borrowed time.

I want a near-death experience tonight. I want my heart to stop beating just so I know what it feels like when it starts again.[95]

.13.6.14.

---

[95] Rehearsed smiles locked tightly within her chest too tight to speak.

For a moment yesterday, I didn't realize I was alive.

It may not mean anything to you, but it did wonders for my psyche.[96]

.30.11.14.

---

[96] The only affectations I leave are subtle and slow;
you may not realize I was there at all until long after I'm gone
but always pulled by conflicting currents
the decisions I make daily corrupt or cradle my ever-changing fate.

<u>Affirmations</u>

Lovers are One
until
they fight.

Marriages work
until
they don't.

Children love
until
they resent.

I am Yours
until
I'm not.

.22.1.15.

Darn Good Soup

Me: this poor human; they've so much going on, how awful/tumultuous
their life
Them: this fucking bitch is everything I hate about the world.

Me: everyone deserves love. benevolence is a duty.
Them: if you "love" more than one person you clearly misunderstand
what love truly is.

Me: I sometimes withhold my opinion because I struggle between
deciphering what I truly feel overall vs. simply how I feel *now* and I
couldn't live with myself if I inadvertently hurt someone by misreading a
scenario without analyzing rhetoric and intention and thus being careless
with my words, triggering a fear or pain I do not intend, as however they
view me, whatever my intention, they are right.
Them: she's ignoring me. she doesn't listen.

Me: in a world where everyone is perpetually & immediately accessible I
struggle with the consistent urge to disappear.
Them: I can't depend on her.

Me: this poor abused animal deserves unconditional love, empathy for
past traumas; I understand. I can help.
Them: she has neither darkness nor depth; it's just an excuse for her to shut
people out.

You: can you ever, just, NOT relive your entire life in every second of
every day?
Me: ...
You: ...
Me: ... no.

.13.5.15.

Piss

I come to this rooftop to come to terms with where I've been.

Five flights of stairs and I've finally given my chest a reason to be pounding but as with anything relative to the workings of my heart it is displaced. The smell of drying piss clings obsessive to my leather soles and, as I sit cross-legged on the edge of this limestone crag, a cadence of distant traffic, idle birds, and the clinking of silverware creates the opus that I can settle into.

The opus, the pulse, just as the heat from the sun on this rock emits an energy, wavers where in the midst of an Impressionist identity edifying this landscape from which I'll be removed, a different sun has set on every part of my face and hands; I can suspend my breath at this altitude to just below that of the temperate diurnal wind as the leaves rustle just as much or as little as my hair to just beyond the edge of me as who I am and who I used to be converges as One Who Arrived and One Who is Leaving, but neither could fit comfortably within each other's reflection and now there is just too much inside.

I come to this rooftop so that the cracks in the street become the Art that reflects my life, that reflects the dried skin between my knuckles in a way the creases within their faces below do not.[97]

The piss, for a second, is overcome by burning meat and hyacinth in a way that isn't entirely unpleasant but I still know that, underneath this bouquet of Spring, the inciting layer of intrigue at this vantage point...

Is still piss.

I come to this roof to refuse anything I might have become other than precisely who I am right now.

But I've come to realize how little I know of who I was at the time of my being.

You can't read the words you write until you've written them just as you can't learn from your mistakes until you've made them but if you could help the ones you love without first understanding how they are hurt then you might beat the Sun before it sets and wait for the Moon to soothe you.

[97] Why can't I see myself in them?

And things might just be different at the moment you look back.

And maybe Lot's wife wasn't a pillar of salt. Maybe she was a person turned to ash that dissolved eventually from the blast of heat from the inferno consuming her suddenly fragile silhouette from her one compassionate moment of loving vulnerability.

And maybe it's God's will to show that the pain we receive from disobedience isn't a punishment imposed as vengeance but merely the natural occurrence from ignoring wisdom we are not ready to accept.

Or maybe it's just geography.[98]

But sometimes I look away from the sun clutching the horizon just in time to see the clouds replace their argent lining for fire and blood reflecting in the empty space of my glasses, the concave observatory of the minutiae, and I can trick myself, just for a second, that I can look back at the ashen remains of my former fire as I feel the heat of the spark forming before me.

I see my past through a camera obscura.

But what a beautiful view.

.29.4.16.

---

[98] I come to this roof to remind myself that at this altitude I'd only feel a brief second of true acceleration before I felt nothing at all.
And I'm not ready to feel nothing at all.

OCCULTUM

Distillation:
the Virgin rises to become one with the Moon,
letting the White Mother descend

<u>0.</u>

If I turn this way
and look into a mirror,
I can almost see myself disappear.

Distilled

Sometimes I love sketching with a shitty pen that leaves the lines incomplete and delicate, like a butterfly tripping over its own inky feet. Making everything I do by accident seem lithe and ethereal in comparison to what I compose deliberately – this suggests that harbouring control like a golden egg is nothing without a trust in my abilities; calm and peace of mind free my faculties more than focused ability ever could.

Confidence is freeing. At the very least there are a few things with which I can rest easy:

.knowing my will is not forfeit
.feeling my drive will be fortuitous

These fleeting fancies and pipe dreams I hold onto when the weight constricts my breath as I press on – ever on – into this tundra of my Unknown.[99]

.25.2.13.

---

[99] (d)riven.

Bad

Happy Birthday, Oblivion. This side racket exit music cutting rights to my vertical film – expenditure and circumstance are breeding bitter moods as ferocity, interned, is misconstrued to pale my eyes.[100]

Without yours, I'd be invincible.

.26.2.13.

---

[100] Some don't understand abuse until it's obvious.

Pressure Release[101]

Waking to a camera flash, you're not really sure if you're alive or still dreaming.

For a few liminal moments you're a teeny martini dancer waltzing precariously on the edge of the glass, eyes flickering in the muted sizzling of champagne pink and golden fireworks. Silhouettes of little eye worms drift, pirouetting in the camera obscura corners of your cornea and float around the room unfolding before you as your eyes struggle to keep up in all those lights, but all you can do is blink. You rub the images in, so they stay, and blink. You take it in, piece by piece. The open window. The edge of the bed – there's a hand there, your hand, bring it to your face as the sounds of the street below creep in muffled like the end of the Brand New record tripping over its own needle. That sound is the sound of the whole world as your mind catches up to the hand on your face. *Your hand.* You focus on your hand, not the room, just your hand and how the hell it got in this room and why the hell is your shirt on the floor, inside out, but all you do is rub it in and blink. Lather, rinse, repeat.

It's called a Pressure Release.

A blood vessel bursting in your sinus cavity – that's it. That's a nose bleed.

The chiropractor pressing so hard into your rotator cuff – you're stuck sandwiched between the chair slammed into your jaw and his iron fingertips slammed into your back – the cluster of knotted muscle separating your shoulder blade from your ribs finally POPs and all that fluid drifts down your spinal cord. He doesn't tell you how far it drifts down or what it seeps into, like a stain on your liver, just drink lots of fluids.[102]

That plane ride yawn where you unhinge your jaw a little and you feel your eardrums recede as the sound of the engine is rushing in, so sudden, so loud in a crash of thunder that stays, you wonder why you popped them in the first place when the dull hum of silence was such a calming sound.

---

[101] [[**Ex/Com**]]**position**

[102] *Some chicks are best consecrated in absinthe and St. Germain; that doesn't mean you have to be.*

Looking up from the bed with a hand on your face – your hand – to see a boy stuffing a Nikon behind his back.

The beads of sweat at the base of your spine.

That sound was the sound of the whole world. The question's out your mouth before you can hate yourself for asking,

"Is that a camera?"

The sound of the street. The skipping record. *Pressure release.* The hand on your face. Your hand. Your world. That sound is the sound of your whole world that was skipping like a record till the needle jumped in a squeal and your hand is the hand of the whole world that brought you here, that hand that's shaking and bleeding when it slams into the mirror that opened the door the hand that tipped the bottle back and that sound is the sound of the whole world so you listen to that sound as you wait for an answer.

As you realize you don't want an answer. You just want to scream. But all you can bring yourself to do at this particular moment is rub it in and blink and see an ashen lady givin' up her vows in the mirror.[103]

You don't even fucking like Brand New.

.19.11.13.

---

[103] What are you that you remain so contained?

Abyssus Duplicata

A broken window, in the end, would ask for nothing but the shards inside the frame, again.[104]

I swear it's true.

The words escape me and I refuse to simplify, but the justice is impartial – I think of nothing, therefore I write nothing. I've grown too impatient for dishonesty. Sometimes, I've heard, it helps to be beautiful. But this isn't that kind of story.[105]

I love pillow talk.

Not flattering niceties of silver-tongued lovers,
but the whispers of those bestowing love and wisdom in the darkness
like waves with secrets content with the moments they've been given to
have conversations that may or may not exist the next day.

It all depends on where the journey ended.
And it's all a matter of when the next journey will begin.

The past comes back to us as an old needle dragged across the skin. That same pain which once filled us with fire, in comparison – it felt shattering in the past – but now it feels dulled. Nullified. Palpable, yet understood. Drag the needle harder; deeper. Just to make sure.

Little vignettes of the past flit by; amazed, you find you're bleeding the same blood you did then.

It's the same pain you felt then. You're just used to bigger needles now.

---

[104] My stretch marks and scars are where I shed my past.
[105] there's a simple pattern in an harmony
that leaves a piece of you deep inside
of me
if I'm too afraid to speak
just hold my hands and in a whisper
tell me

.30.11.16.

Inversions of recall become intravenously palpable. Anything less seems child's play.[106]

.30.11.13.

---

[106] "Daer Patty,
I love the waye I love you and the waye you love me.
Love, John E."

.30.11.10.

I feel drunk and torn within.
I haven't had a drop
yet my stomach's caving inward
like a thief's reflex,
cutting up my mind –
it's nothing but reliquaries in a glass oubliette
that topple and shatter,
freeing each memory in a cloud of smoke
the mirrors devour slowly;
lover's hot breath dissolving in the cold night air –
and I'm caught staring at myself again.
And I ain't a pretty sight, baby.
You're killing me with pride.
I trained my eyes to strain
just a bated second longer,
piercing darkness while I battle dreams
to sacrifice this voice
I've overused
and underrated
now it's nothing but bruised
and I hate each withered syllable slipping out.[107]

I want to battle an empire.
I want to eat bullets and bleed poetry –
don Giovanni trionfante –
and shit putrefaction.
I want to tear myself
from the edge that I'm hanging on,
and pierce through sky;
taste sweet, metallic free fall.
I want something gold to stay.
Just something.

.24.3.14.

---

[107] "Being happy" is a choice I have an incredibly hard time committing to.

The shutdown is a

slow burn out

and a fickle fade away

.1.12.14.

We begin softly
by cheating the sundial
and turning our backs
so the waves never know.

There are faces I've never met
but I see them in dreams
and I'm counting steps
to the exit
without triggering
the coping mechanism.[108]

Music as the only means
to drown out the sound
of my own doubts
laid out ad nauseum;
to memory and alphabetically.[109]

.29.4.15.

---

[108] I don't want to have to defend myself while I'm trying to express how I feel.
It's never up to me, it seems.
[109] Without failing or fronting
I hate who I fear I'll become.

Howl

Even thinking about the word ennui, each noxious syllable of it, leaves a tarnish on my lungs. It's acrid fog on a Spring dawn. A cloud forming in an artist's cornea. A cigarette burn on the 35mm.

Aesthetically, everything is the same. But the imbalance of Form is inexcusable.

I find myself terrified of women whose faces appear to be made of teardrops in sweet descending curvature of æsthetic despondency. As if their noses and cheeks and dying eyes are marooning and dissolving in long and glacial waves of bitter reproach; her cherubic lips are ever-parted but have forgotten the pleasures of sin. The sexless sensuality of it terrifies me. She's a reminder that I could ever forget.

I guess it's time for my confession:

I came here to straddle a dead woman.

It's comforting, in a way, that the dead will never change and in the serpentine dark of this strangling wood the sun fades and I can suck my lip in fits till my mouth is hot copper but my body shivers in this autumnal warmth feeling her chilled skin against mine, iridescent, spilling prisms of light from last night's rain. The few clouds I see remind me that if the wind gets restless it simply changes its skies and that there's a word in the natural world for when you feel you've overstayed your welcome.[110]

I can hear the faint murmurs of a distant orchestra as these shadows cure my contentment with memory. All around me are the shadows of giants that I knew in a distant time in whose hands I left favours of parting from many selves that were once my own.

Before the sun dies, if you look carefully, you can see yourself in every stage of life. They call this the witching hour.

I left you, darling – *I'm sorry* – to walk in orbit around that sundial, thrice widdershins, for the huntress' eye; I kept mine to center as I walked and as I walked I could see my shadow shift and change and if I looked behind I could see who I once was and if I looked ahead I could see who I will be. I don't want to see the shadows of who I am now. The effect I have and the

---

[110] "Dry rot" isn't the right word but it's the first one that comes to mind.

impressions I leave I know all too well; the oily imprints on your neck scream my discontent.

They're why I'm here.

As the light fades the sound of this wood rises and falls in time with my footsteps in the grass and I can smell the sweetness of death in the darkness of the leaves, *la canzone del mio cuore* tremoring in the air as my fingers trace where naval meets breast. The fire of dusk is reflected in the sanguine pool at your feet as I lean in slow to leave the stain of my chartreuse lips upon yours.[111]

I know you understand as I leave you once again that this is the only way that I can keep you.

.11.7.14.

---

[111] The inner machinations of a clock are referred to as "complications."

.petals&thorns.

I just saw a boy who reminded me of you.
All his bags packed with a single rose
and a look on his face that felt
exactly
like we used to.[112]

And that couple there that almost ran out of time
to cross the street because they just couldn't decide
which kiss would be the last.

If I try hard – more than you give me credit for – I can pretend everything
happens for a reason. I have to pretend because I have neither the
clairvoyance nor the faith to truly understand because at the end of the day
I think about all the things I wish I knew and every time it washes over me
in finality akin to the sound a period makes at the end of a sentence; I envy
the lucky ones who still wonder whether they're worthless or not.

I know.
You made sure of that.

.29.8.14.

---

[112] It's not the depression itself; the misery.
It's the fear, the feeling that you're not allowed to have it. That it hurts them, somehow.
.16.5.16.

Night Mare

The storm was old. He could tell by the weight of it. Ubiquitous sound of rumbling from some ancient machine that settles in your joints till you're lead.

New storms will sing to you in their tinny little voices, cradling the trees, lulling you to sleep.

Old storms, though. Old storms come angry, felling branches, splitting shingles, invading every collar; to gaze upward to the sky for a moment is to drown in the elixir of your own hubris. These storms crave the chaos they remember from the sea. Displaced echoes of focused rage lurching forth from the deep coating this world in a salt shit mist as the water rushes in from all sides; a tidal wave that ran out of sand.

They had all the vengeance and cruelty of the bitch that brewed them in the depths of her own misery. Plainsfolk say there's a "Man in the Moon" and a "Man in the Sea." Northerners know better – no man is that capricious. No man would leave a fishing vessel stranded leagues from land in any direction, no wind but ragged breaths straining in the sweltering heat. Three days' catch festering in the sun and that deathly odour driving the crew to homicide as gulls take chunks out of the carcasses & men alike as they can't decipher just who's alive and who's dead.

And you're starving to death so you bite your own lip to keep from screaming. Count how many pints of your own blood you can suck and swallow to keep from dehydrating before their incessant bellyaching becomes an invitation. What man would transform his worshippers into walking corpses then answer their prayers with a tempest? Quench their thirst with mountainous waves, every lurch of the bow the will of the Fates whether they catch the rigging or plunge overboard into the endless night of the sea? Their last breath an invocation of the goddess they believe will welcome them.

A man may give his life to live, to exist within her malignant heart, cruel and remorseless, shriveled to a pitiable shade of himself. But the Moon, the heart of the Sea, that savours each sanguineous pull, the sacred ebb and flow in the soul of men?

Women. Fucking women. The whims of women are the cancer of man; if you listen carefully you can hear her laughter in the eye of a hurricane. The howl of the storm rising out of the waves, cracking of limbs in the sheets of downpour drowning the earth as she spreads her cruelty beyond the boundaries of her waters to punish her children for her own anger; jealousy; fear.

I was a man, once, and I gave my soul for the love of the Moon.

This is the story of how I'm going to kill her.

Vide

Sometimes silence is empty; stagnancy suggesting there once being something no longer hanging on the edge of a current that is now still.

Sometimes silence is palpable; it seeps into the skin protecting an house of bone where inside an infectious heart will wait without beat for answer — or question — to be posed.

Sometimes silence is comfort; the knowing that is selves to one self empowering empathy between two beings that are to just be. Together. *If possible.*[113]

Sometimes silence is orbital;[114] what satellites can say elliptic until need for Language is overcome by a sense that two selves are once more out of sync in need of explanation.

In this cosmic dance we weave through Time foreign to mutual stellar mythos; though constellations coexist only in Silence are we interconnected. Only in shifts are we light enough to speak. This infection without sound is a vacuous impasse once primordial; cruel. In that it reminds us now what we are not.

What we could, by every right, be.[115]

Sometimes, in a tense no other than déjà vu, a Silence occurs that we know we should have already overcome.

Sometimes silence is emrys; occurring just before we realize it should never have occurred.

A silence that is begotten; not made. Our Ascension will come long after armageddon when we find no further occasion to speak.

.20.1.15.

---

[113] Love is the death of Ego and therefore the one thing we fight against most.
[114] Does the heart begin to atrophy after a period of disuse?
[115] In an otherwise well-trained and obedient machine, my heart is the one cog over which I have no control.

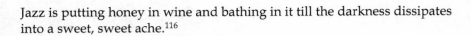

Jazz is putting honey in wine and bathing in it till the darkness dissipates into a sweet, sweet ache.[116]

.30.4.15.

---

[116] There are people for whom loneliness is a disease spread from the consummation of lips and skin and festering within the absence. Machinations whose instinctual urge to explode will not ignite until they are pressed.

Decomposition is our birthright; we have to be entertained.

I do this to myself,

you know.

Days subsisting on fingernails and months composed of shit.

Pissing feels like passing sand.

A current boils through the cold stone evaporating sweat and the

                                                    drip

        drip

                                      drip

                              drip

                                drip

   drip

               drip

                           from above, down to throat to stick to gut

No sound but swelling eyelids licking sight before it cries. Sometime thoughts become sound

          aching ripping fucking silence empty,

                              glass fades churning,

               window behind pulse,

                      light flicker senses flash,

    synapses counteract;

[[*I know you're wondering, but who told you?*]]

Piercing through with needle was easy; in and through and out and through and in and if it wasn't copper wire then it shouldn't taste so much like it is so much like it is so out and through and out and in and seven little pops to keep the thoughts from making sin, out and through and out and in

corruption in the form of: :crying
bile in the form of: :vomiting
blood in the form of: :drinking in
deceptions in the form of: :eating broken promises
begotten :: not

made;

promise to pierce us till we bleed;[117]

I don't...

[[*I don't get out much.*]]

Swinging pendulum bulb ma(r)king time across the walls; I blink. It flickers.

The walls lose track but never let go of the chains

because they're so good

and the chains bleed rust into each open sore and I keep track for them but they tell him anyway and beat me even when I say please...

Wrists should never be that colour.
That rotting metal gangrenous peach.
but the walls stopped caring if I hit them.

Chest pa(i)nting   smells of blood and drool.
        [[*don't say "breasts" or "tits" or "cunt," ok?*]]

Sometimes I try to love myself: kissing shoulders, knees, toes when I could reach – I can never reach my fingertips or feel my eyelashes fluttering against my own cheek.
It's impossible.
That's why I need him.
That's how I know he loves me.

---

[117] I am feeling my own decay; in the eyes and mouth I feel withdrawn from myself.

The sick seeping stopped between my legs after he came and left me last time but thighs coated in milk and blood and stick-sweet smell like angels' fœtid breath and his hands never shake.

He told me this isn't Hell because then there'd be a Heaven and that he could make me sleep but then who would I have to care for and sometimes his lips hover above me and I stare into the space between them as I try to breathe underneath.[118]

Drip. Slip. Drip.

He sliced a little skin off, up and down, so the sutures would knit – cut a little gum too but it grows back if I don't tongue it – my breasts are all swelly swelly belly swelly!

Look:

I am a Venus full of love and my shell is almost cracking to let out my little oyster all over my ocean floor. Swelly belly swelly belly, breasts are swollen pink; he loves me this way.

I know yawning keeps my lips from healing shut but I always fall asleep.

Keep a secret?

I like to sing.

It only kicks when I sing.

.13.8.15.

---

[118] There's blood in the water
and
I'm leaving it there.
I'm soaking it in. I need myself now.
I am all I have.
.10.12.15.

Svblim

There is an ideal precipice from which I could reclaim my faith;

A storm not yet realized rests within this sullen air.

Settling upon this rock, I will wait for this storm to consume me.

Unless I consume it first.

.21.9.16.

I discover my skin when I need to find which parts of me have been left unkempt, fingers pressing into all the places I remember being touched[119] and there is so little give
I wonder why anyone would stay[120]

.17.12.16.

---

[119] Sometimes I can't tell whether it's my skin or my touch that feels foreign.
[120] Temporary dissonance is not indicative of self worth.
Stop isolating yourself emotionally due to preconceived notions contradicted presently, you insufferably loved twat.
... #positiveselftalk

This Town Plays Out in Shifts

– one way in, two ways out;
shoulder to shoulder
but eyes never touch –
in gilded passageways
where people take pictures of shit;
the part you played
you thought would be your last

because
"This isn't real,"

because
"We are obsolete,"

because
"Who wants to live forever?"

is imprinted forever in impartial recognition
where every face
every building
every pigeon on a bridge
is a silhouette in which anything can fit
so you make everything fit
to relate it back to you
an echo to give back to you
to give yourself significance –
everyone knows this
everyone's seen it
and now I'm a part of that;
I'm associated with this forever
and you may never know me and we may never kiss or talk,
one finger each entwined in a secret,
share ice cream as rivulets race through our fingertips
but there are moments in this town that I have crafted carefully
I made so you could fit inside
that will always have a piece of me
that remain only mine until you come into frame.
In that moment you are compacted as your self dwells in my echo
making it new
and you and I transitive in that moment
in that place

we've created the convergence in which we are now everyone.
in every place connected
and now I'll think of you in my city
as I leave lipstick schmeared on borrowed ceramic mugs
breathe smoke till my nimbus bathes me in a scented wreath
the streets will appear in painted secrets
sulphuric low tide heat escaping manholes in bursts
as with me you'll exist in half-held memory
like a poster past showtime
sunbleached with drying tape.

We'll coexist timeless
borrowed songs heard through an open door
And in time we could be everyone
And with time we can be anyone
And in time we will be everyone

I just need you to believe in me.

.14.4.17.

<u>LAPIDEM</u>

Coagulation:
the Phœnix is resurrected as the Ultima Materia

I.

The drums never guided my hips so softly,
so sweetly as pouring milk.
If music did nothing, there would still be these days of Autumn love.

God is in the Rain.

He is pressed into my skin, a barrage, cold and foreign, compared to the furnace inside.

A breath of smoke bleeds into the air, filling the chasmic night – *how can so much escape from these constricted lungs? I am made of fire* – it becomes a cloud, alive, fed by every pull. I exhale in the dark. It is a part of me, extended. The soul I let escape from my heart, burning my lungs, out of my mouth – an offering of fire to the earth and sky.

It is torn apart by the rain.

This is what I have become.[121]

.14.6.13.

---

[121] A man who blames the ocean for the damage of the storm forgets how deeply she must be penetrated for her surface to send him reeling.

.30.5.16.

<u>Ghosts</u>

We're a palpable entity
breaking silence as we move
giving insufficiencies back to every fault that we fill –
goaded into mythos twice distilled to tell us what we are.[122]

We're the pressurized build-up
stored within each heart interred.[123]

We're an aortal aneurysm
pulsing post-mortem.

We are the future.

And this is the American Dream.

.4.4.14.

---

[122] Menstruum.

[123] Be the Lazarus soul you wish to see in the world.

.5.5.16.

Sage

It wasn't a dream of pregnancy; I gave birth to a dream of buttermilk
cradled tight against my chest with eyes of green lazily gazing into me as if
I were Morpheus himself [[I would look back]] before slumber takes her in
my arms I would kiss those eyes a thousand times translucent as they flit
between me and Oblivion –

Daughter I called her. And Sage.

The world became a winter twilight within her Auburn down. Above a
waterfall of light we slowed time.[124] When she fed on me I felt the suction
in my throat and we slept in a bed of lily breath until the dawn.

.23.3.15.

---

[124] Light is the gift from the heavens we receive that enables us to appreciate the natural
philosophy of beauty – we damn this beauty to negative space when we interrupt its rays
with our insidious forms.
.8.12.15.

EOS

I.

The light was warm peaking through the silk curtains
in gentle echo of the Out There through which they drifted;
each moment taken as breath,
an inhalation of silence of the darkness just beyond,
but interrupted
by the glimmer of both distant - & not so - stars.
She watched it creep contentedly
as a brush heavy with paint
bestowing love the only way it knows how when it is welcome,
small shards of crystal capturing every colour
as they dance for her waking eyes
across the marble floor.
The house was a chryselephantine basilica
red velvet staircases and windows holding labyrinthine gardens in place
marble gazebos in the apses
oil portraiture
focusing the eye on the picturesque beauty of trained reality
waiting.

She tip-toed barefoot to the kitchen.

Mama was there sun dosing on the island
her fur a glistening mocha after emptying a freshly picked basket of eggs.
She stroked Mama's back in wait for her to fully wake
feeling the musculature along her spine shudder, her ribcage expand
watching her deeply dive into a stretch
her nails on the marble sound like tap dancing;
she tries to imagine the song.
Eat, child, she hears,
though Mama makes no sound,
as Mama's petite snout sleepily nibbles behind her ear.

Do you like it? What did you see?

"Oh, Mama," she breathes, heart all a-murmur in remembering,
"It was *beautiful*...

The stars swirled and danced and made pillars of light to hold a great blue eye;
I think Orion winked at me.
I blushed.
The sisters swore.
There was an explosion so quiet I had to whisper into my hands.
I felt someone's heart leap into their lips when they were kissed for the first time;
the moon made a song with the waves but the sun didn't notice."

She hung her head wishing the moon knew.

"I bit my lip a little."

Mama smiled.

"I saw a City!"

Mama stopped.

The little hairs along the base of Mama's spine went prickle and up. She had to be careful stroking now so she wouldn't hurt Mama or her fingers. Mama turned and straightened to fill her eyes.

Did you go there?

"Where?"

The City.

She took her eyes away. "No…"

Do not ever.

"But MAMA, lights were flashing by
and hugging black windows stacked upUpUP
and stone there was eaten by metal racers
full of ones and twos covered in ugly fabric clinging ugly
and
some walked in the between of big houses or around and around and around
and some breathed fire but it was so small in their hand
it was just an excuse to draw breath

and some walked in a circle but there were no flowers or music-"

Do not ever go there.

"I just flew right by and they didn't notice
like the stars don't notice
but I brushed one of their cheeks but they didn't-"

I said don't ever GO there.

"… notice."

A long silence passed.
Mama's small teeth ground at the points
and her fluttering heart still fluttering because the silence felt ugly
and she didn't mean it to.

"It was warm."

Mama sighed heavily. *Child, I love you.*

"I know. I love-"

You promised.

"I know."

You promised to monitor the Spaces Between.

"I thought it wouldn't-"

The Space Between happens between Times.

"…hurt."

You must never go to places that stay.
You flow between them and around them and if you don't then you'll stay,
you'll be stagnant in a Place where I can't find you.

Mama nuzzled her but her nose was warmer than normal
and this worried her and she threw her arms around Mama's neck and
cried.
Mama made her eat two berries,

a slice of grain bread dripping honey
and seven whole macadamias
before letting her wander away
and her little tummy gurgled in thanks
as she plodded past the Staircase to where her Favourites stayed.

She held Amphitrite's hand and tried to reach the harpsichord at the same time
leaving footprints on the mirror;
tried to read Apollo's mind but he was distracted
so she giggled with Ganesh.
She stole the nectar from a lily and put it behind her ear,
kissed the petal whispering,
"Now we're one,"
and Lily smiled
nodding gently.
She saw the back of her hand reflected in a silver amphora
and twisted it watching her lithe tendons dance beneath her skin.

She wished she hadn't upset Mama.

Raven told her she was young
but the dolphins in mosaic said Mama was young once, too.
Wolf gave her a light nip when he licked her face
to remind her that Time moved centrifugal
and if you spent too long in one memory
you'd harden Odysseus
till nothing let you laugh anymore.
A gilded sky bled onto the marble.
Enkidu gave her a flower with a look that made her so sorry.
She didn't want to be afraid.
She wanted to know like Mama and she wanted Mama to know she could
find herself if she stayed in Time too long.

II.

That eve she settled back into the Watch Tower,
her nest cold from lack of her.
She took the box from her table and opened it.
That place inside of her trembled
and she glowed in each seven place, *cap à pied,*

and the sound resonated from deep within
like the memory of a bell attaining perfect pitch in echo heard from deep
beneath the waves
and she aligned her breathing with the current between stars
as her eyes rolled black it echoed within her mouth and filled the room
soft and slow till the ceiling cracked and peeled
the walls crashing soundless
as the wake of her song touched everything quaking in the sonorous space
dissembling lines and boundary
all that was a silhouette she felt and made her own.
At once she became everywhere.
She touched a newborn star and said,
"I see you," as a tear fell down her cheek.
She lit the caverns of Moon with laughter and soft whispers from the Sea
and cried silently at the foot of a statue on Mars.
She rode the crest of an asteroid,
ebbing and flowing on currents predetermined
interrupted by imploding decisions
and heard a sound pounding flat against a ring of light.
She tuned it.
She thought of Mama as she drifted through a sun dog.
She thought of City and its ground rose up to meet her,
dark beside the globes of yellow light lining the long stretches of stone
towers of metal and glass
like her Tower
swarmed her taking form rising from below until the towers filled the sky.
She had never seen a sky that could end
transfixed within a realm of finality;
she blamed the towers and whispered to the sky
that her Tower rested on the brief exhale of stars collected by the korai
but it's ok, she decided, because this sky didn't know any better
because this sky was forced to stay.

This City tasted of milk breath and sweat.
An aqueduct held a levitating train
and she walked beneath the length of it
afraid of what might fall from either side.
She walked across the stone and heard voices hidden by the trembling
pillar but a tiny red bug was struggling to wiggle off an aphid
so
the voices had to wait.

They didn't.

The fuck?
Oh my god, is she naked, she's crazy,
She's hot.
Girl be fresh from –
She cold?
fuckin' loony bin.

She knew the voices couldn't be directed at her
which was good,
because she didn't quite understand their dialect;
they covered themselves for a dark masquerade
but a masquerade of villagers on hard times:
The feminine wore plastic tubing in their hair,
neon striped stockings,
dresses ripped about them in strips.
The masculine had black around their eyes,
canines prominent as Wolf's when they talked;
one wore a corset over pleated pantaloons
draped in a floor length black coat embroidered in blue.

A tiny tall glass room rang next to them.
She walked to it
afraid of how quickly her feet moved her away.
Inside she found the ringing receiver waiting to be touched
and when she did Mama's voice exploded in her ear,
WHERE ARE YOU I CAN'T SEE YOU A SUN IN URSULA IS EXPLODI-
and she dropped the receiver
when kohled black eyes with red lashes gaped at her through the glass
lips drawn back in a sneer
and when she leaned in close,
she couldn't help herself,
to gaze at the tiny diamond lodged in an incisor they
CHOMPED
and scared her.
She tumbled out of the glass box.
The feminine touched her hair and she thinks they said,
Finished with your call, sweetie?
but the masculine with the swollen face had touched her arm
and when she recoiled they laughed
and she flung her hands behind her
that someone grabbed
and pulled her so close

a hand greased down her neck
as slow as her stomach churning
and she heard an exhale through the spreading smile
nestled so deeply within the curve of her neck
it left a seething cloud of hot breath inside the concavity of her scapula
that when she threw her head back
she heard a *crack* and then her hair was wet;
she heard the feminine scream
she twisted herself away clutching the hand holding her in hand
afraid loosing her grip would prevent her escape
as if letting go would somehow chain her
until it popped and twisted wrong
and the scream burst louder
and she's never been so scared
and she felt the red wet streaming down her back,
matting her hair as she ran back across the concrete ground
as if it were a river which to cross would mean salvation
and she ran to a door
any door, but she could kiss this door
and she whispered in apology because she didn't have time
and behind this door mirrors and doors to tiny tall rooms perfumed in
excrement
but their walls didn't reach the floor
so she begged them to stretch
and when she climbed inside she heard the masqueraders reveling behind
her.

She latched the tiny hook into the eye
and prayed for silence.
She climbed atop the porcelain bowl.
The door opened.
Footsteps slammed into the ceramic tile.
She thinks a fist hit her only door.
She hugged and hid her face within her knees.
Her door shuddered and a voice said,
Come out here, bitch,
and she shook and shook and shook
"No, no, no,"
into her knees as the fist kept hitting
but this time several fists and they were all talking at her but she couldn't
keep up.

Hey, FUCK you.

Let us in.
Can't believe you did that.
Did you see Nisha's face?
Let's tie her to the tracks.
Where's Bram?
He took Nisha home.
Shit, there was so much blood…
BITCH, let us IN.

And in a silver silence the swollen face appeared beneath the door.

Little pig, they sang,
Little pig,
better let us in
before we three wolves break the mother fucking DOOR in.
she squealed and pushed their face beneath the wall
and it reappeared in the opposite corner
and she struggled keeping her legs close to the bowl while pushing the
face away from her room
and her arms got tired
and her tears created rivulets tumbling through the drying blood
and she couldn't push it fast enough
a hand leeched around her ankle and, pulling, knocked her down
the back of her head burst in a searing pain seeping
and she SCREAMED in aching terror
and when she screamed a light erupted all around her
filling her vision and her mouth
the sound of bone and meat cracking against the concrete wall
fabric ripping as every door splintered
until the tiny room was gone
the white hot fear in her chest became a cavern she sank into
before

nothing.

Darkness.

She didn't exhale.

But the darkness was everything.

III.

She felt the feather down soft of her nest
but she couldn't trust her nest was there
and when she opened her eyes
a gaping maw of jagged teeth roared
spraying spittle that smelled of rotting eggs
and copper that coated her in seconds
and she covered her face with feathers stuck to her hands
and she cried a cry that hurt
consumed within a voiceless scream
because all she knew was crying.

The roaring stopped.
A bleeding snout,
cold and foreign the size of her hand,
traversed her skin and hair and shoulders
hot breath washing over her in spurts.

You smell disgusting,

said a voice like Mama's but low
but angry
but scared
but, how
how could Mama be scared?

She uncovered her face.
Mama had grown to fill her only room,
her golden fur matted and wet
dark as dirt,
dark as blood,
claws protruding from knotted knuckles putting gouges in her only floor.
She wailed and threw her arms around Mama's now grizzled neck,
wracking her delicate shoulders in sobs
and she felt Mama small slowly till she fit her lap
and she stroked her fur
hugged her as Mama licked her face
and arms
and shoulders
and back
till all the blood and salt were gone
and her sobs gave way to whimpers

and the whimpers became sighs,
the sighs replaced with sniffles till the silence filled the room.

When she quieted finally,
Mama bigged again,
just big enough to hold her in her arms,
stroking her hair
talons combing knots
till it glistened pure as the morning dawn would be
if it had no ground to make it stop.

.10.1.15.

Barbed

Night-stalking with an indifferent Atlas – you swear your beauty derives from the burden you bear – each paradigm a sentry we tread beyond in shifts as I trace your body like a silken thread.

Who are we, collective?

Beyond me, cumulative in trans[[c]]ience, we are connected in each wave enamoured with the shore but I keep secrets from myself you uncover as gold, distending each fitful breath I keep within the edge of me, pulling the shards out of every scar.[125]

Who am I, respective?

Within me, there is a resonance your eyes seem to awaken like the gentle wailing of a distant star, that I remember but cannot place as if the memory of you is imprinted but is one I have not yet earned.

.2.2.17.

---

[125] unfolding epiphanies through an obstruction of grief.

Replicvnt

Who are you today?

You don't even know.

You asked a mirror that is too small to contain you and all you can think is that your breasts are too large to wear a bra in public for fear of too many noticing the endowments you never knowingly asked for; the scene in <u>Brick</u> where she monologues idly beside the sound of a fading scale becomes your sole reference for what you've suddenly decided to be your self.

"You weaponize my words," becomes the only mantra you can believe in.[126]

Xeno becomes the husk you fear you'll become.

You are past the point of dread.

These broken words become a reliquary you won't remember in the morning until he remains immersed in the coffee and code that accentuates each poignant flourish he displays to his tremulous screen; in a word, he would charge an empire. In a breath he can seize time. He is not mine, but I would see him æternal – exalted. He breathes me in like a soul sucked through the pipe and when he exhales I become the nimbus existing just beyond others' perceptions as a vapour that is contained solely where it decides to stay; I dissipate as nothing more than a scent seeping into your skin and hair.

I am forbidden without his touch – a fragile placement of glass upon a rough-hewn stone. I am the disturbance of light within his gaze giving pause to an all too iridescent repugnance.

You are an effervescent disturbance to the redundancy of borrowed time.

You are the sound of air escaping.

You are the bruise of Love released.

You are the salve removed from knitted skin; cells reminded of their own completion.

You have escaped the reliquary.[127]

You have escaped the reliquary.

---

[126] I can give you my focus without losing my own.

[127] I slept as someone accustomed to the blood coagulating before it ever flushes out; my dreams reaffirmed what I already know and why I so diligently keep things to myself. The wound will be gone before you take the knife away.

.17.1.17.

You have escaped the reliquary.

You have escaped.

.27.4.17.

It's so hard to forget pain, but even harder to remember sweetness. We have no scar to show for happiness. We learn so little from peace.[128]

---

[128] I think I'm

I know I'm

I used to

I am.

Let's make love like children.

Let's make love like tea leaves in boiled water.

Let's make love like milk and honey.

Let's make love like fingers on taut strings and keys; like lips on the mouthpiece of flutes.

Let's make love like sunlight in a brook babbling softly down a hidden waterfall.

I'll never feel my eyelashes fluttering against my own cheek; you can.

I love you like that.

Try it. It's impossible.

That's why I need you.

That's why you need me.

I need you like I need to write these words and you need to read them.

When you're gone I miss you like the stained glass in a rose window misses the waves...

Made in the USA
Lexington, KY
10 October 2018